Praise

'This book will change your life. *Deep Resilience* will show you how to access an inner strength you didn't know you had, and use it to live with purpose, empowerment and wisdom no matter what life is throwing your way.'
 — **Matt Dickinson**, CEO, *Mindful Magazine*

'If we long to be a force of healing in our world, we must nurture an inner resilience, creativity and open-heartedness. Melli O'Brien offers a beautiful pathway with her Deep Resilience Method – a four-part journey grounded in timeless spiritual wisdom, contemporary psychology, science and her rich experience as an educator and coach. This guidebook, filled with compassion and deep insight, is an inspiring companion for transformation and genuine empowerment.'
 — **Tara Brach**, author of *Radical Acceptance* and *Radical Compassion*

'This incredibly helpful book can truly change your life. Every page is insightful, useful and wonderfully kind. Drawing on good science, spiritual wisdom and her own hard-won lessons, Melli O'Brien is a trustworthy guide to healing the past, living fully in the present and building a better future.'
 — **Rick Hanson, PhD**, author of *Buddha's Brain*, *Hardwiring Happiness* and *Making Great Relationships*

'Skilful tools, transformative practices and wise perspectives, offered with care and heart.'
   — **Jack Kornfield**, author of *A Path With Heart*

'Timely and empowering, *Deep Resilience* blends researched-backed science, wisdom teachings, practical exercises and Melli's experience as an educator and coach. She guides you on a journey from fear to inner strength. This book is a wonderful tool for creating a more compassionate and courageous world.'
   — **Sharon Salzberg**, author of *Lovingkindness* and *Real Life*

'*Deep Resilience* is more than a book; it's a lifeline for anyone seeking strength and clarity in a chaotic world. Melli's ability to blend science, mindfulness and timeless wisdom is unparalleled, offering readers a roadmap to a calmer, more grounded way of being. This revolutionary book will not only inspire you but equip you to thrive in the face of life's challenges.'
   — **Cory Muscara**, author of *Stop Missing Your Life*

'This book will transform your life and help you face whatever arises with courage and care along with mental and emotional strength. It is borne of Melli's many years of research and practice and her exquisite sensitivity to how we can thrive as individuals through following her simple and

powerful Deep Resilience Method. It is also a profoundly generous book, and Melli's wish for collective thriving shines through on every page. She has written this book as an act of love for the world.'
— **Vidyamala Burch**, author of *Living Well with Pain and Illness* and *Mindfulness for Health*, and co-founder of the Breathworks Foundation

'Grounded in science and illuminated by spiritual wisdom, *Deep Resilience* offers a revolutionary framework for cultivating inner strength. This book is a lifeline for anyone seeking not just to survive life's challenges, but to thrive through them with grace and authenticity. This book doesn't just teach resilience; it feels like a companion guiding you gently back to your true self. It's a precious gift for anyone seeking hope, clarity and the courage to navigate life's storms.'
— **Jo Wagstaff**, author of *Lead Like You*

'If you or someone you know is facing difficult times, this book is an essential read. What truly sets it apart is its unique blend of cutting-edge science and profound spirituality. Melli's approach is both grounded and deeply uplifting, making the wisdom she offers accessible to all. The result is a toolkit for cultivating resilience that feels both practical and transformative. Deep resilience is not just a concept – Melli shows that it's something anyone can build, no matter where they are on their journey. I highly recommend this book to anyone seeking lasting strength and timeless wisdom to navigate life's challenges.'

— **Shamash Alidina MEng, MA (Ed)**, author
of *Mindfulness for Dummies*

'Discover the power to transform your life and the world around you in this deeply moving and profoundly insightful book. With clarity and compassion, it guides you to the very essence of what it means to be human, offering wisdom that is both accessible and transformative. Let this be your guide to unlocking the potential within you to create change – from the inside out.'

— **Mark Coleman**, author of *Awake in the Wild*

'*Deep Resilience* is a powerful guide to navigating life's toughest challenges. I love the blend of practical skills, scientific insights and timeless wisdom. Melli O'Brien offers readers a pathway to rediscover their inner strength and thrive in the face of adversity. Her compassionate and deeply personal approach make this book not only inspiring but also a great toolkit for cultivating resilience, clarity and purpose. A must-read for anyone seeking to rise above life's difficulties and embrace their most empowered, authentic self.'

— **Elisha Goldstein**, PhD, author of
Uncovering Happiness

DEEP RESILIENCE

A FOUR-STEP JOURNEY TO
UNSHAKABLE INNER STRENGTH

MELLI O'BRIEN

R^ethink

First published in Great Britain in 2025
by Rethink Press (www.rethinkpress.com)

Contents

Introduction

You are strong. Even if you don't feel that way right now. It may be that the challenges you're facing are dragging you down, draining your vitality and eroding your hope, despite your best efforts to soldier on, push through or think positively.

But no matter where you find yourself or what you're going through, no matter how lost, afraid, confused, exhausted or overwhelmed you may feel, there is a reliable and profoundly transformational pathway back to the strength within you.

In the last fifteen years of working as an educator and coach in the mental health space, my courses, retreats, coaching and app have helped over a million people globally. I've taught mindfulness and mental strength skills to people around the world, from different cultures and backgrounds and all walks of life. I have had a front-row seat to observe the patterns that help and those that harm us in difficult times, and I have seen, over and over again, that the difference between whether we will tip into struggle, disempowerment, despair and defeat or whether we will remain resilient, empowered, wise and effective in the face of our challenges boils down to four key skills.

I have distilled and carefully crafted these four skills into a reliable and transformational framework that I call the Deep Resilience Method. It is a four-step pathway, combining cutting-edge evidence-based mental strength skills with spiritual wisdom, that has helped thousands of people revolutionise their state of mind in hard times so that they are no longer governed by fear, reactivity and stress and are instead guided by calm, resilience, love and purpose.

I have seen how this method has allowed people to unlock their greatest inner resources, enabling them to handle challenges effectively, create positive and lasting change and find peace, healing and meaning in the middle of it all.

This book will put you on the road back to that strength inside yourself. It will reconnect you with what's deepest, strongest and best in you, and bring you home to your true self.

There is no golden ticket for getting through life without adversity. In our brief time on this little blue planet, we experience moments that are unbelievably beautiful, and others that are unbearably painful. The challenge is that most of us have never been taught how to deal effectively with the whole of this reality – especially the really hard parts.

It could be a relationship breakdown, an illness, a devastating failure, the death of a loved one or financial troubles. Maybe it's an internal battle with loneliness, addiction, anxiety, depression, low self-worth or trauma. When those blows hit, as eventually they will for all of us, sometimes we stumble and lose our balance and other times we fall. As we shall see, what happens next is what matters.

If you are struggling for any reason, if you need to find solid ground, then this book is for you. Inner strength is the most important thing in a person's life. You can't always count on the world, other people or even your own body, but you can always count on your deeper nature and the inner strength inherent to it.

The Deep Resilience Method has helped parents and caregivers, CEOs, changemakers, activists, athletes, entrepreneurs, students and many others from all walks of life to find their mental, emotional and spiritual inner strength, and it can help you too.

By the end of the book, you will have taken your own personal journey to deep resilience. You will have become someone who, when faced with pain, fear and difficulty *responds* to it by tapping into some of the greatest capacities and strengths innate to the human spirit instead of *reacting* in ways that cause you to suffer, become disempowered, defeated or debilitated.

You're not alone in needing more inner strength right now.

The World Health Organization estimates that mental illnesses such as anxiety and depression now affect one in eight of the entire global population,[1] and more than a quarter of Americans say they are so stressed they can't function properly in daily life.[2] More than 75% of people under thirty report feeling daily anxiety about the future,[3] and depression is now the leading cause of disability in the world.[4]

In just the past few years, we've faced a global pandemic, growing recognition of the impact of climate change (including unprecedented bushfires, floods and storms and significant changes in weather patterns), international wars, a cost-of-living crisis and rapid changes to technology and the world of work. All this is on top of the personal challenges we all face in the normal course of life.

That is a lot to carry.

I am struck, these days, by how many of my clients tell me they are unhappy, struggling to cope and feeling disconnected in the present, and are also feeling a sense of foreboding about the future. There is a widening gap between the fulfilling and happy life they wanted to live and the one they are, in fact, living.

This is why, after many years of working with people from around the world, I am now writing this book. While I continue to take as many people as I can through the Deep Resilience Method individually, online or in person, there is also an urgent and growing need to share this knowledge more widely. These skills are no longer a luxury; they have become a necessity. The challenges we face ahead are growing fast and we need to grow in response.

The Deep Resilience Method

The Deep Resilience Method evolved over many years of teaching both mindfulness and mental resilience skills to people all around the world, through retreats, courses talks and coaching, and by going through my personal journey. It is a cutting-edge psychospiritual framework that combines elements from the evidence-based fields of mindfulness, emotional intelligence, peak performance psychology, neurolinguistic programming, stress-reduction tactics and positive neuroplasticity training, and integrates them with core components from the world's wisdom teachings. It brings together everything I've learned from my own lived experience, modern resilience research, coaching, teaching, testing and consulting with experts, and distils it down into four basic components that are intricately linked and in some ways inseparable. Together, these four steps form a fitting acronym: RISE:

- **R = Recognise and Regulate.** By learning to manage thoughts skilfully and regulate emotions in healthy and helpful ways, we step out of the turmoil of suffering, stress, hopelessness and fear and shift into empowerment, peace and confidence. We open up the mental space to find our centre and strength again.

- **I = Inhabit the Present Moment.** Through mindfulness-based practices, anchor yourself firmly in clarity, stability and the wisdom of your deeper nature and let it lead, allowing you to respond more wisely, authentically and effectively to whatever challenges you face.

- **S = Stay Connected to Your Values.** Rather than being pushed around by stress, fear, negativity and anxiety, be pulled by your values. This switch gives you an unshakable source of inner purpose, empowerment and resilience. You may not be able to control what happens to you, but you can always choose how to respond, led by your values.

- **E = Engage in Empowered Action.** Empowered action is action guided by presence (outlined in Step 2: Inhabit the Present Moment) and purpose (as described in Step 3: Stay Connected to Your Values). In difficult times, engaging in empowered action will move you from feeling overwhelmed, anxious or helpless to instead feeling calmer, more confident and in control. In this step, you bring your inner strength to the outside and make real meaningful changes in your life and in the world.

All of the above steps are intricately linked and contain elements of the others, which you may notice as we work through the method, but each focuses particularly on honing a particular key skill. By building yourself a foundation of deep resilience, you'll be able to:

- Revolutionise your state of mind by skilfully handling your thoughts, massively reducing stress, anxiety and suffering

- Regulate your emotions in healthy ways so you feel calmer, more confident and connected to purpose

- Heal and transform unhelpful thinking patterns, letting go of limiting beliefs, unwinding feelings of unworthiness and self-doubt, and relieving stress

- Unlock your potential so you can be the parent, partner, leader, changemaker and person you want to be

- Perform at your peak, even when under pressure and stress and in times of conflict

- Reconnect to the innate wisdom and wholeness within you

- Connect to a greater sense of belonging, meaning, fulfilment and purpose

- Take effective action to improve your situation, allowing you to feel more empowered and in control

- Find freedom and peace of mind in the middle of it all

- Awaken higher and deeper potentials in yourself

This book does not claim to be a panacea for everything. It cannot take away your difficulties, magically solve all your problems or erase all of your pain. What it can do is help you unlock your inner strength and rise to whatever you're facing with the best of who you are, providing you with a reliable pathway to effective action, purpose, meaning and inner peace. This is the promise of the Deep Resilience Method.

The book is divided into two parts. The first part of the book is about building mental and emotional strength and outlines the key concepts that together comprise the first step of the RISE framework, which sets us up for the steps and work that follow. The other three steps form the second part of the book, which is about building wisdom (spiritual strength). The principles outlined in this book have stood the test of time and the scrutiny of science. They have created real, documented change in many people's lives, including my own.

My story

I came to this work because I was desperate for help. By the age of seventeen, childhood trauma, a troubled family life, the pain of not fitting into the school system and living in a world that felt insane had eroded my self-worth and hope. I was grappling with self-loathing and a deep, existential and profound grief. I had sunk into depression and developed an eating disorder. I tried therapy and other healing modalities, but nothing changed. *Life is way too painful. I can't go on like this; it's just too much,* I remember thinking. I could see only two options: take my own life or try one more time to find a way through to a new one. This last-ditch effort transformed my life.

Through research and practice, drawing from various approaches, traditions and teachings, I discovered that I could train my mind to do things differently and that inner strength was a *skill* I could develop.

This was a game-changing realisation.

I now understood that change was possible, maybe even inevitable. Just like learning to ride a bike, drive a car or the steps of a dance, with enough repetition and practice, I could develop a stronger, happier, calmer mind, so I threw myself into practice.

I practised meditation every day; I broke unhelpful thought patterns; I developed new inner skills and strengths. Within a few months, I saw drastic changes. My eating disorder alleviated and then disappeared and so did the depression; neither have returned. The circumstances of my life also improved quite dramatically, and over time, I began to experience even more positive changes and realised there was a whole other way to live in this world. A whole different – and more fulfilling – way of being.

I have since dedicated my life to this work. Over the years, I've helped over a million people globally through my courses and retreats. I also co-founded Mindfulness.com and The Mindfulness Summit, the world's largest mindfulness conference. Through these projects, I've donated over $750,000 to mental health charities around the world, and I am honoured to have been named one of the most powerful women in the mindfulness movement by *Mindful* magazine.

My big vision is to make the world mentally stronger so we can work together to solve our most meaningful problems and create a more sustainable, equal and peaceful planet. Sharing *Deep Resilience* is a central part of that mission. My life has been profoundly transformed by these practices and I can see the promise that it holds for us collectively.

At the same time, I am still learning and practising these tools every day. I stumble, I fall, I try again. I'm walking this path along with you and I still have a lot to learn, but I'm 100% committed to the path of deep resilience.

If there is one tip I would share to enable you to get the best out of your investment in the pages to come, it's that knowing something conceptually is not the same as experiencing it directly. Conceptual knowledge may be interesting, entertaining or even inspiring, but ultimately it won't be liberating. True change comes from doing. By applying these practices and experiencing them for yourself, change, transformation and liberation can take place. To that end, I encourage you to put these skills to work in the laboratory of your own life as you read. Find out first-hand what benefits they offer – how they affect your body, your mind and the quality of your life.

I encourage you to experiment, explore and find ways to make these practices your own. If something doesn't resonate, don't worry. I recommend just giving them a try a few times so that you get a chance to experience the results for yourself – and if something doesn't feel useful or helpful, just leave it. There are various tools on offer in each step, so test them out and take from this book what works best for you.

Whatever you've been through in the past and whatever you're facing right now, these tools will help you find your strength again and rise.

PART ONE

UNLOCKING MENTAL AND EMOTIONAL STRENGTH

1
How Did We Get Here?

I remember the moment when the realisation hit me like a ton of bricks.

It was dawn on a perfect winter day, and I was sitting on a chair on my balcony. The sky was erupting with colour, the sunlight's warmth made contact with my skin and the birds were starting to chirp, but I felt numb to the beauty and light around me. It all seemed somehow distant, like I was seeing it from behind a screen.

I hadn't slept all night. In fact, I hadn't slept well in weeks. I felt wired but simultaneously desperately and deeply tired and getting more so by the day. I felt a heaviness was sinking into my bones, like a fog rolling in, like a light inside was being dampened and extinguished. I hadn't been able to focus or perform properly at work for some time and I had to take leave from co-running a company that I founded and dearly loved.

After going through the breakup of a nineteen-year relationship, the deaths of two loved ones in close succession and a painful social conflict, all in a short space of time and while running a busy start-up company, I had developed debilitating mental and physical symptoms that progressed into a mysterious chronic illness.

With my health now rapidly deteriorating, I felt like everything had been stripped away from my once-golden life, and now even my ability to do the thing I loved and gave so much meaning to my life – helping others – was disappearing.

Preceding this series of painful events, I had been on a roll. I felt like I was at the peak of my career. Doors and opportunities were opening for me, I was doing work I loved, and life felt full, fun and meaningful. I was living in my dream home, nestled into a tight-knit family and friend group. Everything crumbled so fast.

Emotionally I felt like a combination of a zombie and an ant under a magnifying glass. Sometimes feeling searing emotional pain and at other times feeling so totally empty, tired and foggy-headed that I couldn't do much at all.

I'd experienced pain in my life, like most people, but what I had been through before was meagre compared to this. I was on my metaphorical knees.

And that's when it hit me: the realisation. Here I was, a mental health educator on the brink of breakdown. Shame rolled in like a gathering storm. I felt like a shadow of myself, and a fraud.

What followed soon after, though, was curiosity, and the question 'How did I get here?' Of course, I had been using mindfulness and mental resilience skills to help me find relief and strength through this time. These helped me to find greater peace, at times, by letting go of everything and resting in a deeper place within myself. At other times, these tools helped me remain non-reactive, grounded and able to navigate the deep exhaustion, the overwhelming pain, the hard conversations and the crashing waves of fear, with some compassion, ease and equanimity. Mindfulness especially, was a source of deep healing and a place of refuge.

But the realisation that became exceedingly clear to me on the balcony that day, is that the tools I had in my toolkit (the same ones I had been teaching to others for years), were not enough to unlock all the inner resources I was looking for in that moment. I needed something more to stay empowered, effective, wise, strong and loving in the face of this kind of adversity. I needed a reliable, accessible and robust framework to access the deeper strengths and resources inside me and stay anchored to them as I navigated my way through it all.

A troubled world

This period of my life was incredibly humbling and at the same time, deeply insightful. It brought my life to a full stop. That gave me the opportunity to turn, face and deeply contemplate something else that had been weighing heavy on my mind and in my heart in the past years.

The world had changed a lot since I first started teaching, and in many ways, not for the better. The demands, complexity, uncertainties, disconnectedness and difficulties of modern life were growing exponentially. In fact, it seemed like the world was reaching a tipping point. All at once we were experiencing a climate crisis, a mental health crisis, a technological crisis (with people racing to create AI while simultaneously warning us of the existential danger of doing so), a geopolitical crisis (with wars breaking out and countries' increasing militarisation) and a cost-of-living crisis. It was getting harder and harder to thrive and be happy in what Dr Gabor Maté calls 'a toxic culture'.[5] A culture constantly pushing materialism, consumerism and individualism as the highest ideals for our lives, despite decades of research showing that these pursuits don't make us happy, whole or high functioning.[6]

I had been hearing from the coal face how people were feeling more overwhelm, stress and anxiety and less hope and optimism. Many clients reported feeling a loss of meaning, disconnection and disempowerment in the face of the world's new challenges. Then when they also experienced their own personal troubles, these were compounded by the background radiation of stressors, the challenges of modern life and the state of the world.

In light of all this, I had been holding another question in the back of my mind for some years:

How are we as a collective going to rise to this?

How can we unlock what's best, strongest and wisest in human nature so we can work together towards that vision of a peaceful, equal and flourishing world? Returning to my own dark night of the soul, I held that question and context close to my heart and in my mind as I worked to find a solution to the problem of how to find our greatest inner strength through our personal adversity.

I started to deconstruct and analyse my own firsthand experience. I compared it with the gold standard, cutting-edge research on resilience. I dived deep into wisdom teachings and mindfulness practices. I consulted with thought leaders, coaches, therapists, researchers, monks, swamis and scientists. I interviewed people who I knew had overcome incredible adversity and were inspirational examples. I self-experimented some more and have since refined my ideas and techniques through work with clients over these past years, looking for the common threads, seeing what worked and distilling things down to the most reliable, transformational, evidence-based tools and skills. Through this, I found the elements of a robust framework for accessing and embodying our deepest and most reliable inner strengths and highest human potentials.

This is how the Deep Resilience Method was born. I developed it, not only because it was what I needed at the time, but also as my way of responding to the changing needs of my clients and to meet the times we're now living in. It is a practice to soothe our pain;

to untangle us from being stuck in our stress, fear and confusion; to reclaim our power and reconnect us to the unshakable source of wisdom, love, courage and strength we all have within us.

This method has helped me and many others to find our centre, rise to our challenges effectively and find peace, meaning and freedom in the middle of it all. And for me, and again many others, deep resilience has become a way of living.

How do we start on the path towards becoming resilient? We begin by understanding how we all got here in the first place.

Downwards spirals

The unfortunate reality is that when life gets painful, messy, scary and difficult, most of us don't deal all that well with it. Because of the way the human mind is wired, we can easily get hooked by scary, negative and painful thoughts and emotional reactivity, and then get stuck in loops of the same repeating patterns for days, weeks, months or even years.

These patterns can drag us down, disempower us, hold us back and pull us into unhelpful behaviours. For example, we might lash out at the people around us, numb or distract ourselves with alcohol or drugs, over-working, food or TV, withdraw from our loved ones or stop doing the things that nourish us, make us happy and fill our cups. We might give up on our hopes and dreams, neglect our health, hide away from the world, or perpetually distract from our challenges, spending hours shopping, scrolling social media or staying busy. We might just straight up refuse to get out of bed.

All of these kinds of behaviour are normal and natural ways of coping with stress, uncertainty and pain. Almost all of us will display them to some degree. The problem is that when they become your ongoing way to deal with difficulty, they make things worse, drain your resilience and prolong your distress rather making things better, increasing your resilience and promoting healing, recovery and flourishing.

Although it might be our mind's default mode to try and manage our pain and difficulty in these ways, the great news is that we can change any of our unhelpful reactions to new, life-affirming and empowering *responses*. We can rise to our challenges, but first it's important to understand how we got here, into this state of struggle, in the first place.

The reality is that when we're hit with hard times, we face an additional challenge. As we learned above, the human mind tends to react automatically in ways that amplify rather than ease our distress. These reactions can pull us into a downward spiral, add even more suffering and distress, diminish our inner strength and tip us into a state of *fear*.

What is FEAR?

Over the years of research, working with clients and using these tools myself, I have come to see clearly that the great majority of the time, the biggest source of the struggles, suffering and disempowerment we feel in the face of hardship, is not the situation we face (and this is not in any way to minimise the severity, tragedy or injustice of what you might be facing). It is the FEAR our mind tips into in response.

The acronym FEAR describes the four specific reactions to pain or adversity that take away our power and amplify our distress. They are:

- **F – Fusion** with thoughts

- **E – Engaged** in a struggle with our emotions

- **A – Actions** that are draining or disconnected from our values

- **R – Remoteness** from the present moment – therefore losing touch with the wisdom and strength of our deeper nature

Fusion with thoughts

It's normal and totally natural to have a certain number of negative thoughts in hard times, but many of us get stuck in a loop and end up *fusing* with them. We worry, overthink, ruminate and fixate. Our mind often starts spinning and racing frantically. When we fuse with thoughts – that is, when we get caught up, hooked on, or buy into them – we greatly amplify our distress and suffering. We end up unwittingly drumming up more fear, reactivity, anxiety, disempowerment, stress and insecurity.

Overwhelmed, many people then try to get relief from their racing thoughts by trying to push them away, fight them off, drown them out, ignore them or paint over them with positive thoughts, but these strategies are not helpful.[7] In fact, they are detrimental. These common strategies to deal with unwanted thoughts tend to backfire and cause the amplification effect, a well-known concept in psychology, which in essence means that when you try to get rid of thoughts, they will tend to get louder, repeat themselves more and stay around longer.[8] This creates the perfect conditions for a downwards spiral of mental turmoil. As each negative thought arises, we amplify and fuse with it in ever-increasing cycles of distress and exhaustion.

What we often don't realise is that it's not the thoughts themselves that are the problem; it's the *way we relate* to them. This pattern of fusion with thoughts, and then the struggle to get rid of them, is common and it ends up piling more layers of stress and anguish onto an already painful time, clouding our minds and diminishing our ability to respond effectively and recover.

Engaged in a struggle with emotions

In difficult times, we are likely to experience painful emotions and stress. That is a perfectly natural result of going through something tragic, difficult, frightening or painful. The idea that we should not feel emotions like sadness, anger, fear or grief during these times, or that they are a sign of weakness, or that there is something wrong with us for feeling them (an idea that is sometimes promoted in the media, personal development books, and even by medical professionals) runs totally counter not only to the research on resilience and mental health, but also to basic human biology.

Any healthy human being will likely have an influx of difficult thoughts and feelings in response to life stressors. These could include feelings like anxiety, sadness, anger and fear, thoughts of worry, self-criticism, hostility, self-doubt, rumination and regret. This is our minds and bodies doing the job they were designed to do: responding to the surrounding environment, attempting to signal important information to us and motivating us to take action to stay safe and healthy.

Although a certain amount of stress and strong emotion is normal, we can easily tip into unhelpful reactions. Often, we can get locked into a struggle with emotions or end up totally overwhelmed, engulfed and overtaken by them. We may become reactive, disempowered, depressed or totally consumed by fear, anxiety or hopelessness. Swept up in their powerful currents, it can be hard to find solid ground again.

Similarly to thoughts, many people try to manage difficult emotions by pushing them down, ignoring them, battling against them, drowning them out, or perpetually distracting themselves. As with thought suppression, attempting to suppress emotions too can lead to the amplification effect. Suppression of emotions has the same effect as thought suppression – it makes them louder over time and inclined to stay around longer, and it can even lead to mental illness and symptoms of physical illness.[9]

Often, emotional suppression involves the adoption of unhelpful ways of coping, such as substance abuse, disordered eating, overspending and overwork, to name just a few, and these ways of coping lead to other problems in our lives. Our emotions and bodily sensations also hold valuable information about our needs, our values and what is good (or not good) for us in our lives. Suppressing them can mean you miss important signals and signs that help you navigate life in helpful, authentic and adaptive ways.

Actions that are draining or disconnected from our values

During difficult times it's common to neglect our health and wellbeing more than usual and stop doing a lot of the things that energise us and bring us balance and happiness. In short, we end up doing more things that drain us and fewer things that sustain us. Over time, this depletes our reserves. It can result in brain fog, exhaustion, burnout and breakdown, as well as anxiety, depression and health problems. This impacts everything from work performance and sleep quality to relationships and overall life satisfaction.

While it's totally understandable to want to withdraw from hobbies and social contact for a while, to take the edge off, find relief or cope by staying distracted, working or eating comfort foods occasionally, the problem begins when we start to make these ways of coping our default, ongoing mode for dealing with pain, stress and fear.

When we're stretched to our limit, we also risk becoming reactive instead of responsive. In reactive mode we may lash out, make decisions or take actions that we later regret, and we're not as effective at making decisions and taking actions that are helpful, skilful and wise. We may lose sight of our values and what matters to us deep in our hearts and/or start acting in ways that are unhelpful (for ourselves and others) and out of alignment with who we are deep down. Not only can this leave us feeling more drained, disconnected and depleted in the short term, but it can also lead to deeper unhappiness both in the present and in the future as we gradually become more estranged from our authentic selves and the things that really matter and give life meaning and richness.

Remoteness from the present moment

When we are swept up in all the inner turmoil caused by fusion and struggle with thoughts and feelings, we become more and more *remote from the present moment* – and therefore awareness itself. This is problematic for two main reasons. First, because without awareness we tend to stay stuck in FEAR-based patterns. Awareness is what gives us the power to pause, untangle ourselves from thoughts and emotions and then consciously choose new, more helpful ways of thinking, living and being. Without awareness, we have no choice but to unconsciously play out our mind's conditioned patterns.

The second problem is that when we lose touch with the present moment, we lose touch with the greatest source of inner strength we have as human beings: awareness and the qualities that come with it, like love, inner peace, equanimity, clarity, wisdom and courage.

Awareness, or what I often refer to as the deep self, gives us a refuge of inner calm, steadiness and wholeness. It is a bedrock of inner strength and deep wisdom. This allows us to access the greatest resources of the human spirit, those that will empower us to face our challenges and rise.

If we become lost in the turmoil inside our heads, it is easy to end up feeling totally cut off from our strength, agency, innate wholeness and wisdom. We can lose our centre and get stuck in confusion, overwhelm and stress. On the other hand, if we can regain our ability to be present, we can reconnect with the power within us. Through awareness, we can step out of reactivity and struggle and choose more helpful, adaptive and effective responses.

The practice of inhabiting the present moment is more commonly known these days as mindfulness. Mindfulness involves maintaining a moment-by-moment awareness of the 'here and now' experience with openness, curiosity and a lack of judgement. During turbulent and stressful times, mindfulness becomes like an anchor that can hold us steady in strength and wisdom so that we don't get swept up in the stormy seas of emotion, confusion, suffering and fear.

Are you in a state of FEAR?

Over the years, I have noted some tell-tale signs of being in a state of FEAR. People tend to become **drained, distressed, disempowered** and **disconnected from meaning**.

Drained

As you get yanked around by swarms of racing thoughts and strong emotions you gradually become worn down, both mentally and physically. You could then find yourself more tired, reactive and moody, and less able to cope and respond well.

Additional energy-draining actions and coping patterns may further deplete your reserves over time. These might give a little relief in the moment, but ultimately, over time they erode your vitality, mental clarity and strength even more. It's common to push the body and mind to keep going even though our system is crying out for rest.

It can become a downward spiral. As we get worn down, the racing thoughts get louder and the exhaustion deepens. We often keep pushing through instead of resting. This then ramps up our stress levels, further increasing reactivity and anxiety. Brain fog starts to set in, you start to lose performance at work and your mood slowly slips into darker places. Your unhelpful coping styles ramp up in response, and on it goes. Day by day, you're losing vitality and mental clarity, and if nothing interrupts the pattern, it can easily slip all the way into burnout and breakdown.

Distressed

Even though you may be completely exhausted, you're also in an ongoing state of elevated stress – wired but tired. You may be able to put your game face on and tell everyone you're OK, but on the inside, you are feeling an almost constant barrage of stress. You might feel insecure, anxious, agitated, angry, bitter, resentful or depressed, or be struggling with self-doubt or low self-worth.

You may find yourself ruminating and fixating on your problems, regrets and grievances and finding little to no enjoyment or contentment in daily life. Sleep quality starts to decline due to the racing thoughts and elevated stress, so you find yourself tossing and turning during the night, then feeling more tired and having trouble concentrating the next day.

When we're stuck in a state of stress, and our fight or flight system kicks in, we're likely to become reactive instead of responsive to our situation. It's hard to think clearly and rationally in fight or flight mode, so we may find ourselves lashing out, doing and saying things we can later regret, making unwise decisions and being rigid and inflexible in the face of difficulty.

This state of reactivity makes things much harder in both the short and long term, often creating conflicts, draining our vitality and blocking our ability to find creative solutions, foster understanding and look for positive ways forward.

A background of low mood, reactivity or high anxiety can become the norm after prolonged stress. Coping behaviours set in to manage your state but these only work for a short time and then the stress returns and the cycle repeats. After a time, you may find that the ongoing stress takes a toll on your mental and physical health and has detrimental effects on the circumstances of your life such as your relationships, business, career or performance.

Disempowered

In a state of FEAR, overwhelm or apathy (or both) in the face of your challenges are common. You may feel powerless, disheartened, lost, confused, unable to cope or even hopeless. You may settle for situations and circumstances you don't really want, feeling like there's no use trying to change things.

Clients describe feeling defeated, crushed, beaten down, lacking in certainty and confidence. In its essence, being disempowered means feeling a lack of agency in your life and losing the confidence that you have the inner resources to make helpful changes and navigate your life in a life-affirming, effective and purposeful way. When disempowered, people sometimes give up on their meaningful goals, become apathetic, feel like they are stuck or that things are hopeless. In response, some just stop caring about anything; others, in more extreme cases, may even think about taking their own life.

Sometimes disempowerment happens because people feel victimised, seeing others or external circumstances as having done this to them. They may feel robbed of their power and unable to heal, change and thrive again. They may get stuck in blame, resentment and depression. Some say they feel broken, stuck or unable to move forward.

It's easy (and understandable) to fall into a disempowered mentality when you get hit by painful, difficult, unjust or even tragic events. However, it's not useful or helpful for us because in this mindset, our ability to heal, to rise to our challenges, grow and take back our power, is inhibited. Stuck in disempowerment, we underestimate, overlook or forget how strong we truly are. We give away our power and our potential is stifled.

Disconnected from meaning

In times of challenge or difficulty, we all too easily lose sight of, and lose touch with, our values, the goodness in our lives and what matters most to us. Instead, we become bogged down by our problems, distracted by our difficulties and pulled under by our pain. We can become more and more engaged in coping behaviours. We often lose touch with the deeper dimensions of our being and the feelings of happiness, contentment, wholeness and calm that are innate to it.

When we overlook the things that used to bring us fulfilment, purpose and joy, and stop giving our time and energy to the things that truly matter to us, we can often start to feel that life is lacking meaning, that it has lost its beauty, richness and fullness. Instead of enjoying life, we simply cope or go through the motions, just putting one foot in front of the other. We get lost in being busy. We are living, but we don't feel truly alive. As one client of mine expressed it, 'Life just starts to feel "meh".'

FEAR is a downwards spiral

What I have come to see clearly after years of work in the field of mental strength is that when we remain stuck in FEAR, we don't coast along. We tend to head in one definite direction: down into deeper suffering, disempowerment, exhaustion and stress. The longer you stay in this state of being, the more it tends to wear you down, increase your suffering and stress and sap your inner strength, and the harder it is to find the way back.

Every domain of life is affected when you remain in a state of FEAR. You can't perform as well at work, relationships suffer, your health (both mental and physical) depletes, your mood plummets, your challenges are harder to navigate, and your important goals become harder to reach. Your potential and power are stifled, and you may feel that the person you wanted to be and the life you wanted to live are slipping away.

We've probably all met someone who went through a crisis, loss or difficulty and was never the same again. Maybe it's the person who went through a divorce and became bitter and jaded, and gave up on relationships for good; the person whose business failed, who then gave up on their dreams and became depressed; the person who suffered a big misfortune and lost that sparkle in their eye and the easy laughter that used to characterise their way of being.

While the circumstances may differ, the common root cause for many folks is that they found themselves pulled unknowingly and innocently into FEAR. They simply didn't know what was happening. They slid down the slippery slope, got stuck down there and haven't yet found their way out again. If only they knew that they were only a few simple steps away from taking their power back, finding relief and regaining a sense of fulfilment, purpose and meaning in their lives.

The Deep Resilience Method

At any given moment, no matter who we are, where we've come from, what we're dealing with or what we've been through, we can change direction in a heartbeat. Once we make the decision to shift from living in FEAR to strength, we kickstart a virtuous upward spiral that begins with finding rapid relief from our stress and suffering and then, step by step, leads us to living in a state that I call 'deep resilience'.

What is deep resilience?

Deep resilience is a state of mental, emotional and spiritual integration and strength. In deep resilience, you are able to:

- Regulate your thoughts in skilful ways (mental strength)

- Regulate your emotions in helpful and healthy ways (emotional strength)

- Act with awareness and according to your values, even when it's difficult to do so (spiritual strength, or simply 'wisdom')

After many years of teaching and coaching, it has become my firm belief that in order to unlock our full potential and inner strength we need to develop all three of these strengths in tandem. Developing mental and emotional strength alone (which is a commonly taught approach in the mainstream approaches to mental health) is not enough and to me, is not true inner strength. Without wisdom we humans often deploy our mental emotional strengths and skills in ways that lack true insight into, and alignment with, our own nature and our connection with life, each other and our planet.

If we have emotional strength without wisdom, we are like a ship without a rudder; there is a lot of power, clever technology, movement and action, but these can all take us way off course. Ultimately all that power will tend not to take us to the right destination (happiness, peace, love, wellbeing for ourselves, others, the planet, etc) unless we also have wisdom. In this way, it is the most important of the three strengths, and we tend to get lost and stray from our true course without it.

Even so, if we only focus on developing wisdom on its own without also building strong mental and emotional capacities, we may fall short of being able to actualise our wisdom in our day-to-day lives. This can be frustrating for many people who have highly developed wisdom but see a big gap between what they know inside and what they are able to embody in their lives. For example, a person may struggle to regulate their emotions and be caught in reactive or addictive patterns despite being strong in their capacity to embody mindful awareness. Mental and emotional strength help us to transform unhelpful mental, emotional and behavioural habits, skilfully navigate external challenges, unlock our potential and enhance our relationships, work, wellbeing and ability to be a part of making positive change in the world.

How do we get to deep resilience?

The key to entering and acting from the state of deep resilience is accessing and integrating all three strengths and being able to do so in a simple and reliable way.

The antidote to living in FEAR is to RISE through the four steps of the Deep Resilience Method. These four deeply transformative steps, which we will walk through together in this book, will enable you to gradually take back your power and tap into an inner strength and peace that you can access in any situation or circumstance. The Deep Resilience Method will equip you with a powerful and practical toolkit that you can call on for the rest of your life. You can use it in your personal life, your professional life, your love life and your spiritual life.

The situations you face going forward may not always be within your control, but you can always RISE to them from a place of deep resilience.

Step 1: Recognise and Regulate

In this first step, we are focusing mainly on developing mental and emotional strength (although, as mentioned, all steps are intertwined), the ability to adapt and respond to thoughts and emotions in helpful and skilful ways. It starts with recognition. Like the vast mass of the iceberg that sits below the surface, we are often not aware of the bulk of the mental and emotional patterns that are leading us into troubled waters.

To change these patterns, we have to see what's there, so we can then learn how to work with it in new, more helpful ways. It's very difficult, if not impossible, to change something you aren't even aware of.

Recognising these patterns is the first step towards becoming deeply resilient.

Suppressing, being overtaken by, or struggling against our unwanted thoughts and feelings is not productive or beneficial; in fact, ultimately it just hurts and hinders us more. To regulate them in more effective ways, we need to learn the right skills and tools.

One meaning of the word 'regulate' is to bring something into balance so that it can operate properly. This is an apt description of what we will be doing with our mind in this step: training it to come into balance so it can function more effectively and stay healthy and strong. Using mindfulness-based skills, we will learn to let go of unhelpful mental and emotional patterns and instead intentionally shift our focus to more empowering and helpful patterns that help us to feel better and thrive.

In the Recognise and Regulate step, we disentangle from our racing, scary or unhelpful thoughts. We learn to calm the storms of emotion and find our centre and stability. Our mind clears and our body calms as we come into inner balance and restore energy and vitality. We begin to feel more at ease and empowered and we start to act more intentionally, authentically and effectively in the face of our difficulties.

While this first step involves developing mental and emotional strength, allowing us to unwind a lot of the stuff that holds us back, drags us down and causes us excess suffering and stress, it also makes way for the next three steps of the method, which allow us to tap into our wisdom and the greatest sources of inner strength we have as human beings.

Step 2: Inhabit the Present Moment

In this second step, we use mindfulness-based skills to further calm and centre the mind and simultaneously create the inner space to connect with our deeper nature and its enormous reservoir of strength, calm, wholeness and wisdom.

As we have seen, it is the basic pattern of being pulled into and then pushed around by FEAR that saps our resilience, disempowers and drains us, and causes us so much distress. It keeps us locked in reactivity.

What would it be like if you were able to let go of living in fear and its offshoots like stress, anxiety, greed, scarcity, hopelessness, hostility, pessimism and shame?

What if everything you said and did was motivated by love, confidence, wisdom, courage and a clear sense of purpose (qualities that arise when we are connected with our deepest self)?

Consider the way you have that difficult conversation, make the big decision, face that challenge, make the changes you have to make, conduct yourself at work and home. What if, through it all, you were unshakable in your ability to harness this kind of inner strength?

This is the promise of deep resilience. Through inhabiting the present moment we learn to let go of

FEAR and galvanise our connection with our deeper nature. We let it take the lead so that we are no longer governed by fear but instead guided by purpose, awareness, wisdom and strength.

Step 3: Stay Connected to Your Values

When FEAR arises, it can be a powerful force that can all too easily destabilise us, so we need something else, a stronger foundation to stand on. By staying connected to our values, we are pulled by purpose instead of being pushed around by fear.

Values are like the foundations of a house. The house is you. A house built on a solid foundation will be stable and steady, even in the most turbulent storms and wildest winds. But a house built on a weak foundation will start to break down and fall apart when bad weather hits. In fact, even in easy times this house will not be very strong and may start to crack. You too will feel stable, strong and resilient through the ups and downs of life if you are built on the solid foundations of connectedness to your values.

Values are inner qualities that you believe are important in the way that you behave and live. Examples of values are things like kindness, loyalty, generosity, compassion, adventure, playfulness, grit, love, family, fairness, wellbeing, mindfulness and so on.

In the midst of chaos and difficulty, if we are able to stay connected to our values we can act intentionally, moving forward in our lives with a sense of empowerment, certainty and clarity about who we are, how we want to act and what matters most in life. In my work over the years, I have seen that the ability to stay connected to your values is one of the strongest predictors of resilience through difficulty.

It is common to lack clarity on our values. It is easier to identify what we want to avoid or escape than to pinpoint what exactly we *do* want. This comes down to not knowing what our values are; we must identify these in order to build a strong foundation that can see us through hard times.

In this step you are given the tools to become crystal clear on your own core values, on what you stand for and what matters to you the most, enabling you to live a more purpose-driven life.

Step 4: Engage in Empowered Action

Decades of psychological research shows that our life satisfaction, our ability to stay resilient in the face of fear, stress and sad experiences, depends not so much on how many difficult things we experience or even their intensity, but by the way we deal with them.[10]

Empowered action, the final step of the process, brings the whole Deep Resilience Method together and allows you to *respond* to what happens around you in a way that uplifts and supports you and allows you to thrive.

Empowered actions are actions that are guided by 'presence and purpose'. That is, when taking empowered action, you're acting with awareness and according to your values. Staying focused on what you can control, who you want to be and what matters to you, and taking empowered action gives you the ability to be responsive; it allows you to let go of reactivity, victimhood, hatred, hopelessness, fear and greed, and carve a clear path forward with wisdom, power, purpose and intention.

FEAR, then, does not define or defeat us – we choose our response. Engaging in empowered actions means we can reclaim our agency and tap into resilience no matter what is going on around us. This leaves us better able to show up as our best selves and stay in our power in the middle of it all.

Deep resilience in practice

Fundamentally, the Deep Resilience Method is mindfulness-based resilience training interwoven with the cutting-edge skills and tools for self-mastery and resilience. It is both a macro practice and a micro practice. As a macro practice, by building and applying these four skills habitually in your life, you will develop optimum mental fitness by integrating mental-emotional-spiritual strength into your bones and being so that you carry this strength within you wherever you go, no matter what happens. In this way, deep resilience becomes a more enlightened, authentic and empowered way of being and living. It is an ongoing path towards unlocking your deepest strengths and highest potentials.

It's also a micro practice, meaning that when you face a challenge, you can move through the four steps below to unlock and activate your deepest resilience in that moment. A tough conversation, the moment you hear bad news, a setback on the way to a big goal – when you meet any type of struggle, you move through the steps. It can take as little as thirty seconds once you are familiar with them.

As a micro practice, Deep Resilience is available to you in four simple steps, RISE:

- Step 1: You **Recognise and Regulate** thoughts and emotions in a healthy and skilful way.

- Step 2: You **Inhabit the Present Moment**, grounding your attention in a place of inner clarity, wisdom and steadiness.

- Step 3: You **Stay Connected to Your Values**, so that you can respond with purpose instead of reacting.

- Step 4: You **Engage in Empowered Action** (if action is needed) from a place of connection to both presence and purpose.

As a micro practice, the Deep Resilience Method offers a reliable and supportive framework to lean on in the tough moments of life.

There is no issue too small or large. You can use the RISE steps when faced with minor challenges like traffic jams, missed trains, small setbacks, conflicts and disappointments. It's also robust enough to guide you through the darkest, most difficult and overwhelming moments of life.

Practising these skills regularly in less difficult situations will strengthen and embed the method deep inside so that it will be there for you as a bedrock of strength when the big challenges hit.

Deep resilience is a practice, but it's also a state of being. Use the four steps again and again so that it becomes like a strong inner muscle and eventually deep resilience will become your default mode, changing from being a passing state you occasionally tap into to being a lasting trait. It will become who you are and define your way of being in the world. With time and practice, your ability to access that source of inner strength will become more and more effortless, just like riding a bike or driving a car. It will become easier and easier until you don't have to think about it anymore. It will become an ingrained and fairly effortless skill, allowing you to meet what arises with the best of who you are.

Summary

The Deep Resilience Method will take us from a state of FEAR:

- Fusion with thoughts
- Engaged in a struggle with emotions

- Actions that are draining or disconnected from our values

- Remoteness from the present moment

Into a state of integration and inner strength, through the four steps of RISE:

- Recognise and Regulate

- Inhabit the Present Moment

- Stay Connected to Your Values

- Engage in Empowered Action

By becoming deeply resilient we stay mentally, emotionally and spiritually strong no matter what is happening, and find power, purpose and peace in the middle of it all.

2
Step 1: Recognise
And Regulate

The ability to recognise and regulate your thoughts and emotions is the critical first step on the journey towards becoming deeply resilient. This is because it holds the key to unwinding the grip of FEAR and opening up the space for us to tap into our inner power. In this book, it is where we will spend the largest part of our time, not because the subsequent steps are any less important, but because we have to first attain the ability to free ourselves from the patterns that are keeping us stuck in stress, suffering and disempowerment before we can solidify our ability to stay rooted in the greatest strengths and potentials of the human spirit.

'Know thyself.' These words were inscribed prominently above the entrance to the Temple of Apollo at Delphi, a sacred site in Ancient Greece. Many great teachers throughout history have asserted similarly that knowledge of the self is the foundation for human flourishing. We start our journey with the ability to know ourselves and our minds better.

It's very difficult, if not impossible, to change something you aren't even aware of. Conversely when we recognise a pattern, it starts to lose its hold over us and we are able to then use the right skills to work with it in new, life-affirming ways.

That's why in this chapter, we start with learning more about your mind.

The human mind is a double-edged sword

Any writer (or reader, for that matter) knows the power of a hook. It's that moment in any good story that captures the audience's interest and ensures we stay engrossed in the story for as long as possible. Once hooked, the emotions, longings and tensions of the characters become ours, and the more compelling the drama, the more deeply we're drawn in.

We may not all be Hollywood screenwriters or Pulitzer Prize-winning novelists, but each of us has a mind that's constantly generating mental scripts and inner narratives that have an incredible capacity to hook our attention and draw us into drama, emotional reactivity and inner turmoil. These stories can also skew our perceptions and even make us lose sight of reality entirely.

Getting hooked, in this sense, is not like enjoying the excitement, romance and action of a good movie or book. It means becoming entangled in unhelpful thoughts or emotions that sap our mental strength, disempower us and ramp up conflict, stress, confusion, negativity and fear.

Through learning how to unhook ourselves we can radically change our relationship to thoughts and emotions. We can learn to recognise the unhelpful narratives created by the mind and shift them in more empowering directions as needed. We can learn healthy and helpful ways to work with difficult emotions and 'anchor' ourselves in more resourceful and empowered states.

In this chapter, you will gain insight into the nature of the mind and begin to form a new, wiser and more adaptive relationship with it. You'll start to practise some effective strategies for regulating your thoughts and emotions so that you feel more centred, more confident, more resilient and more whole.

From your own worst enemy to your greatest asset

Your mind can be your own worst enemy or your greatest asset. If you're like most people, you will at times have experienced both of these realities. But a lot of the time, the mind can feel like it's working against you: don't worry, it's not just you!

The truth is that your mind means no harm and is just trying to help (as we shall see), but it needs your wisdom and guidance to regulate and train it. To do this, we need first to learn how to recognise how the mind operates, and where and how it gets you hooked in unhelpful ways.

The human mind has incredible strengths, but it also has a dark side. On the one hand, the human mind is responsible for much of our incredible success as a species. With it, we can dream up goals and ideas and map out the steps towards achieving them. We can think about the past and learn from it. We can figure out solutions to complex problems, like curing illnesses, creating cities, roads and railways, put humans into space and build spaceships that can land on Mars. The mind is capable of truly incredible things.

Unfortunately, having a human mind comes with a downside. These same abilities that have led to such success are also the cause of the great majority of our stress and suffering. The mind can haunt our inner world with hurtful words that can crush our self-esteem, drive us into depression or cage us in limiting beliefs. Its narratives can ramp up feelings of stress, hostility, scarcity and craving and keep us stuck in loops that make life harder and disconnect us from our deeper wisdom and higher potentials.

Why should it be this way? It all has to do with evolution. Because of the way the human mind is wired, it constantly plays out and draws us into specific, predictable conditioned thinking patterns. Once you understand the nature of your mind and gain the right skills to work with it more effectively, it can become your greatest ally and asset in both good and hard times.

By befriending your mind and learning to meet it with understanding, wisdom and skill, you will be better equipped to regulate your thoughts and emotions skilfully and without getting hooked.

Wired to survive

The human mind is a meaning-making machine, operating from a foundation of primal survival-based programming.

At any given moment, your mind is taking in vast amounts of sensory data from the external environment and trying to figure out what it all means and what you should do in response. As part of its way of doing that, it generates a continual internal narrative. It is always commentating, speculating, judging, criticising, analysing, predicting and making stories out of experiences: *I am Melli. It's time for breakfast. I need to eat something healthy. Let's make a smoothie. Here are the ingredients. I'm going to start work early because I have a lot on today. I need to dress warmly because it's a bit cold today…* and so on. This ongoing mental dialogue has a purpose and that is to make sense of and navigate the world in which we live.

Estimates vary on exactly when Homo sapiens (modern humans) evolved but it is generally agreed to be around 300,000 years ago. For most of human history, our ancestors lived as hunter-gatherers.[11]

It's only been in the past few thousand years that humans started creating more complex civilisations, and only the last fifty years or so that we've led our particular kind of busy modern lives. A blip of time in the larger scale of human history. This means that our minds have mostly evolved to adapt to the savannah rather than the city.

Hypervigilance

The lives of our early ancestors were hugely different from ours today. For them, life was perpetually difficult and dangerous. To survive, they had to be hypervigilant – that is, continually on the lookout for potential threats, problems and danger. Those who were constantly alert and quick to react to any unexpected sounds or sights were the ones who escaped the predators – they were the ones who survived. The ones who weren't? Well, they didn't survive long.

The default setting of the human mind is safety and survival above all else, so even if hypervigilance made our hunter-gatherer ancestors feel constantly on edge, anxious and stressed, that would have been an OK price to pay – better to be alive and stressed than dead.

In the early days of human history, a hypervigilant mind was an evolutionary advantage. Enhanced vigilance increased the chances of surviving long enough to reproduce, as the mind issued a constant series of alerts and alarms: *Look! What is that over there? That shadow in the forest might be a member of a rival clan coming to attack you, so you'd better get ready! Careful! That rustle in the bushes could be a predator coming your way!*

Back then, heeding these internal alerts was a good idea.

Even though we now live in a totally different world, our mind still operates in much the same way, but it now tends to fixate on different problems and perceived threats like your relationships, work, finances, health and so on: *Hey, watch out! You didn't get that paperwork right; what if you lose your job? Careful! Your partner isn't looking happy; what if they leave you? Quick! That thing on the news says trouble is coming; you'd better get ready!*

It was a helpful survival strategy in the past, but now this constant hypervigilance and tendency to fixate on worries and problems creates a lot of unnecessary and excessive tension, anxiety and unhappiness. It gives us restless nights, stress-filled days and can truly suck the joy out of life.

Negativity bias

The mind has an inherent negativity bias. That is, it tends to dwell on what's wrong more than what's going right. Again, this comes back to our primitive drive towards self-preservation: to survive, it was vitally important to quickly identify and react to negative experiences, so that we could outwit predators and avoid danger.

Imagine if Great-great-great-great-great-great-great-Auntie Mabel stepped out of her cave one morning and looked out across the landscape. On one side, she sees a rainbow and on the other, a dark shadow. Mabel needs to focus quickly on that dark shadow, quickly ruling out a potential threat before then turning to enjoy the beautiful sky. By first focusing on the potential threat or problem, Mabel's mind has ensured she is more likely to live to see another day – and another rainbow.

These days, this inherited negativity bias means we tend to focus way more on what's wrong than what is going right in our lives. We remember insults better than compliments, focus on our flaws more than our strengths, stew on our problems more than recognising our good fortune, remember painful or negative experiences better than positive ones, and think about bad things more frequently than good. This is true both in the way we think about ourselves and the way we conceptualise other people and our interactions with them. We are more profoundly impacted by negative events than we are by equally positive ones, and, when making decisions, we place greater weight on negative than on positive information.[12] Mabel's negativity bias ensured her survival, but for us today it can cause a lot of undue stress, pessimism, misery, resentment, disempowerment and even depression.

Insecurity and unworthiness

In the early days of human history, we only survived in tribes. Getting kicked out of your tribe meant certain death as it wouldn't be long before a predator, a rival clan or the harshness of nature got hold of you. Staying alive depended on fitting into the group and having the approval of others.

To ensure our survival, the mind is wired to continuously monitor whether you have the approval of the tribe members. To do that, it runs an ongoing process of evaluation and assessment: *Am I fitting in? Am I contributing enough? Am I special enough? Am I of value? Am I attractive enough? Am I following the rules? Am I doing anything that might get me rejected?* It also constantly compares you to everyone else and tries to measure your usefulness, status, specialness, abilities and attractiveness against theirs. If you feel you have the approval of others or that you are 'better than' them in some way, you feel safer, more confident, more at ease. But if you perceive that you're falling short you may feel insecure, unworthy and stressed. Others' 'betterness' can be seen as a threat, and you may even resent them.

This aspect of the mind also comes to life in a form commonly referred to as 'the inner critic' – that harsh inner voice that puts you down, points out all your flaws, tells you you're not enough as you are and that you need to prove your worth in the eyes of the tribe or the world.

Most of us don't live in tribes anymore but our minds are still running this old operating system. Our minds are still assessing and appraising our worthiness, constantly comparing ourselves to others, filling our heads with negative self-talk and compelling us to push our bodies and minds to their limits to show we are 'worthy' of approval and acceptance, that we are lovable and valuable to others within our tribe. This was great as a strategy for survival in days gone by, but in our modern lives, it can leave us with a constant feeling of unworthiness, insecurity and depression.

Even more challenging is that, in the modern world, this aspect of the mind is easily aggravated, for two reasons. First, many people are living disconnected from a true sense of having a tribe – a sense of deep belonging and connection to a close-knit community (which ramps up the mind's fear circuitry) – and second, we also have something our ancestors did not – media and the internet. As we scroll, surf and click, we are constantly exposed to airbrushed, polished and perfected images and stories of people who seem better looking, more successful, happier, wealthier and 'better' than us. Our primitive instincts kick in and the mind can't help drawing comparisons and assessing whether we are 'good enough' and we end up feeling that we are falling short of those impossible and often artificial standards, exacerbating our feelings of isolation and unworthiness. Subconsciously we anticipate rejection and threat. This is a pattern well known to marketers, who take advantage of this tendency of the mind and then offer their products as the solution (buy their products) to feel better.

Rumination

Have you ever found yourself replaying a painful or embarrassing moment over and over, each time leaving you feeling worse and worse? Perhaps it was spilling a drink all over yourself at a party, or a careless comment you wish you hadn't made. Maybe you berate yourself, going round and round in loops, thinking about what you wish you had (or hadn't) said or done and you just can't let it go?

This sort of rumination had its uses in the past. If a hunter-gatherer had a run-in with a predator and managed to survive, their mind would replay the event over and over so they could learn everything they possibly could about how to survive the next encounter. That memory contained valuable information that had saved their life once and might do so again, so it is scoured for any and all useful information to remember.

This thinking style is useful to a point in our modern lives, but left unchecked, it just results in shame spirals, sleepless nights, stress, overwhelm and anxiety. Long past the point of learning anything helpful for the future, we get stuck on endless replay and those memories become fodder to reinforce self-limiting judgements, negative beliefs and unconscious biases (more on those later).

Unhappiness and craving

Resources were scarce in days gone by and the minds of our ancestors would fixate on getting more resources and improving life circumstances: *You need more food, you need more water, better clothing, better weapons, better shelter...* More, more, more.

This tendency of the mind still persists within us and now manifests itself as a constant sense of dissatisfaction with what we have and a craving for more. Sometimes it arises as a 'scarcity mindset', the feeling or sense that there isn't enough to go around so we need to keep working hard and hustling to acquire things and increase our power and wealth even when we have plenty. No matter what we get, do or achieve, the mind keeps telling us it's not enough. We constantly want something different, something more, something better, and we can get stuck in an endless cycle of always seeking pleasure, power and certainty but not finding any lasting satisfaction or fulfilment.

We get stuck in a rut of endless craving. For some, this is felt as a background restlessness, emptiness or sense of unease. For others, it looms larger as a deep pervasive unhappiness and a strong sense that something is missing or wrong with their lives.

On top of all of these challenges, our mind also grapples with limiting beliefs, has unconscious biases that skew our perceptions and cause us to become defensive and aggressive, and we get stuck in patterns of resistance that amplify stress in difficult times.

The mind in overdrive

Here's the kicker. All of these inherited conditioned patterns in the mind are greatly ramped up when we are going through a challenging time. When the mind senses difficulty, uncertainty, change or pain, these survival-based patterns tend to go into overdrive. They are patterns that evolved to protect and serve you, but that's not what they're doing now. Faced with modern challenges, these thinking patterns instead lead you to become *more* self-critical, anxious, defensive, stressed out and negative just as times are getting tough and you need your inner strength the most.

During these times our mind often comes up with narratives that can:

- Convince us we are unsupported, unseen, alone, inadequate and unworthy

- Heighten our anxiety and distress

- Debilitate us with limiting beliefs

- Make us reactive, leading us to do and say things we may later regret

- Cause conflict and drama in relationships

- Make us feel powerless, stuck, out of control and hopeless, a victim of circumstance

- Lead to unhealthy patterns of behaviour and reduced self-care

- Degrade our mental and physical health

Our minds generate stories and judgements all the time, but it's during hard times that we need to particularly watch out for its tendency to create unhelpful thinking patterns. These are the moments when we're more vulnerable to being hooked in by the high drama, fear and tension, making our life even harder than it already is.

Being stuck in a state of FEAR makes these survival-based patterns run at a fever pitch. This hijacks our ability to think clearly and rationally and limits our capacity to act intentionally and regulate our thoughts and emotions in healthy and helpful ways that help us to heal, thrive and make positive changes. If we stay in survival mode for too long, we eventually start to lose touch with our deeper and greater human capacities for wisdom, courage, wholeness and love.

When your mind is doing all this unhelpful stuff, just remember that it's not just you – this is what human minds have evolved to do and we're all in it together. It's not personal and there is nothing wrong with you. When we first begin working together, many of my clients often judge themselves harshly or think something is wrong when they feel themselves falling into these patterns. I explain that this is simply part of the package of being human, and if anything, it just means that their mind is particularly good at playing out its survival patterns. If you tend to think like this, you would have been a superior survivor in the hunter-gatherer days!

These kinds of narratives and mental-emotional patterns are understandable and natural responses, especially in times of stress, pain and uncertainty, but they are also not helpful or useful in the majority of the situations we tend to find ourselves in now, and that's why it's so important to become deeply resilient. Instead of letting these FEAR-based patterns dominate and take control, deep resilience will allow you to tap into your strength, calm and clarity when you need it most.

Right effort

In Buddhism, there's the concept of 'right effort' that the Buddha asserts is critical to becoming enlightened and ending suffering. He explains that it's not just effort applied indiscriminately, but the *right* effort applied in the right way to bring about your desired result. Diligent efforts applied in the wrong way ultimately fail to bring liberation and end up draining energy, causing frustration and can often end up deepening suffering and stress instead of alleviating it.

This same principle can be applied to resilience. When people are struggling, suffering and disempowered, it's usually not through lack of effort that they tip into more overwhelm and suffering. On the contrary, all too often (and I've seen this many times with people I've worked with), they are actually trying incredibly hard to push through, keep their chins up and stay positive, but their efforts to stay strong are not the 'right effort'. Their strategies are weakening them instead of making them stronger and it's like struggling in quicksand. The harder they try, the deeper and more quickly they sink into overwhelm, exhaustion and fear.

One of the challenges they face is that a lot of mainstream advice on resilience is unhelpful and some of it is even downright damaging. It's easy to understand how people can be drawn into trying unhelpful strategies. Social media is awash with witty and inspirational-sounding posts that, with the right images and soundtrack, can easily go viral despite spreading bad advice. I have seen TV presenters and even some personal development books recommending ways of staying strong that run totally counter to the evidence base and human nature. Much of this advice, when applied, makes things worse. Even well-meaning friends may echo those same sentiments, saying things like:

- 'Just get over it.'

- 'Stop worrying about it.'

- 'Stay busy!'

- 'Just think positive and it will be OK.'

- 'Don't be so negative.'

- 'Get rid of your negative thoughts.'

- 'Push through it!'

- 'Don't let it get to you.'

Many of these statements minimise the reality of what it's like to go through incredibly painful, heartbreaking or challenging things. They can stifle healing and growth and disconnect us from our innermost resources, and in many cases, cause people to feel ashamed of the reality of their thoughts and feelings.

Have you ever tried 'to just get rid of' unhelpful thoughts, or to switch all your unwanted thoughts for ones you prefer? Did you just try to push them from your mind and plaster on a happy face? Stuff them down and try to forget about them?

We all try to regulate our thoughts and emotions in some way, but a word of caution: not all methods of regulating your thoughts are helpful; some don't work at all, and some are harmful. There are some common myths I've come across about how to be resilient and get through hard times; let's look at a few of these now.

Myth 1: Just think positive

'Being positive has become a new form of moral correctness,' says Harvard Medical School psychologist and bestselling author Susan David in her 2017 TED Talk: 'We are expected to go about our lives thinking positive thoughts and projecting positivity. But "negative" emotions are part of the human experience, and they only become more amplified when ignored.'[13] David argues that society has taught us that negative emotions should be avoided and suppressed in favour of 'thinking positively', but that allowing and being able to work with emotions, even those that are challenging, is necessary for a full, meaningful and fulfilling life.

Of course, thinking positively has its place (which we will get to later in this book). It's great to take time to focus your thoughts on gratitude and to see the goodness in the world, yourself and others. A generally positive outlook in life is a helpful thing, but trying to cope in stressful times by just forcing yourself 'to think positively' is rarely successful. The reason for that is that, in reality, our 'positive thinking' often takes the form of denying or suppressing thoughts and emotions we don't like or want to get rid of, or simply pretending everything is OK, or debating, arguing or fighting with your mind.

For instance, when your mind says, *This is a disaster. You made an idiot of yourself and everyone hates you now*, you might reply mentally, *Don't say that! Everything is great. Love and light. Let's focus on the bright side.*

No, it's not, your mind retorts, *That thing you said was so stupid. You're an idiot.*

You reply: *It's FINE! It was totally fine! Stop saying that. Let's focus on the positives!*

Your mind reasons back: *Look, if everything's fine, why did that person not call you for a week?*

On and on you go, round in circles in a debate you can never win.

There is also the danger of toxic positivity when we start to develop an unhelpful fixation with, and reliance on, pleasant thoughts and emotional states. The underlying assumption is that no matter how painful, tragic or difficult a situation is, we just need to employ a positive mindset and everything will be OK. In reality, some experiences, situations and emotions are simply extremely challenging. Sometimes we are genuinely not feeling OK and acknowledging that can be the beginning of healing and change.

It's a lot to ask of yourself or anyone else – to pretend to be happy, always look on the bright side, or just get over it, even when hit with a big stressor, grieving or profoundly heartbroken. When we demand positivity from ourselves or others instead of offering understanding and empathy, we can make ourselves or them feel stigmatised and judged and deny the reality of those emotions.

Toxic positivity suppresses authentic emotional expression, demeans the reality of grief and suffering, and makes people feel under pressure to hide their true experiences. The reality is that part of what it means to live a wholehearted, full and meaningful life is allowing ourselves to experience the full spectrum of human emotions. Research shows that in the harder times, we need tools other than just positivity if we are to remain resilient, healthy and effective – things like self-care, self-compassion, mindfulness and the ability to reach out for support.[14]

As researcher and author Brené Brown notes: 'what we know now is that when we deny our emotion, it owns us. When we own our emotions, we can rebuild and find our way through the pain.'[15] Accepting (or 'owning') all of our emotions, even those that are difficult or painful, is, Brown argues, the way to regain our sense of agency, enabling us to better heal, grow and 'find our way' forward with wisdom and courage. Positivity has its place, but in times of hardship we are better served by other tools as our predominant ways to regulate, stay strong and cope.

Myth 2: Get rid of your negative thoughts

Ignoring, stuffing down or pushing away difficult thoughts makes them louder and more pervasive. There's a whole field of study dedicated to the paradoxical impact of thought suppression – ironic process theory – and even a term for the phenomenon: ironic rebound, also known as 'the white bear effect'.

In 1863, Russian writer Fyodor Dostoyevsky wrote an essay that would fuel studies on thought suppression many years into the future. In 'Winter Notes on Summer Impressions', he set his readers a challenge: 'Try to pose for yourself this task: not to think of a polar bear, and you will see that the cursed thing will come to mind every minute.'[16]

Over a century later, social psychologist Daniel Wegner read Dostoyevsky's essay and was intrigued. Wegner and his team at Harvard University asked a group of students to do exactly what Dostoyevsky had asked of his readers: try hard not to think of a white bear. For five minutes, the students reported all of their thoughts. If a white bear came to mind, they had to ring a bell. A second group was told instead that they *should* think of a white bear all they wanted for five minutes, again ringing the bell whenever they did so. After five minutes, the two groups swapped.[17]

What happened next has since become one of the most widely replicated results in the field of psychology. Over the course of many experiments, Wegner identified a concept he called 'ironic process theory', meaning that the more forcefully you try to push thoughts away, the louder they become, the more they repeat and the longer they stay around. In other words, when you try to suppress a thought, you actually get more of that thought than if you didn't try to suppress it in the first place.

Dostoyevsky was right. If we try not thinking about a white bear, the cursed thing will indeed pop into our minds more than ever. The same applies to any thought.

When we have unwanted or unhelpful thoughts, all too often we end up doing exactly the thing that makes it worse, and the harder we try to suppress them, the stronger the rebound effect.

Here's the key takeaway: thought suppression has a paradoxical countereffect. If we try to manage our stressful thoughts by avoiding them, it will backfire and land us with more stress. If we try to manage depressive thoughts by getting rid of them, we get more depression. If we try to manage our negative thoughts by pushing them down, they will break through in ever greater numbers. You get the idea.

Myth 3: Soldier on

Soldier on. Keep your chin up. Push through it. Keep on truckin'. Toughen up. Get over it. No use crying. Got to get on with the show.

We've all probably heard these kinds of encouragements, whether in person from a friend or in the media. I remember growing up here in Australia, there was this ad on TV where people were encouraged to 'soldier on' with a cheerful song that told them to take a particular medicine when they have the flu so that they could avoid needing to rest or take time off and continue their busy lives and get everything done.

This sentiment of soldiering on may sound like a form of mental toughness when promoted by upbeat commercials and charismatic motivational speakers, but in reality, it all too often takes the form of stuffing down our thoughts and feelings, putting on a smile, pretending everything is OK, using coping behaviours to get through the day and ignoring our body's signals that we need rest, healing and extra support. What often looks like toughness on the surface is a slippery slope down to disconnection from ourselves, our feelings and our needs. Over time, it can lead to mental health problems, burnout and physical illness.

While of course we will need to attend to some practical aspects of our lives even when we are hurting, overwhelmed or exhausted, the idea that we can act tough, push through it with grit, not show any vulnerability or 'weakness' and keep going about life the way we always do, is often unrealistic and subverts our ability to remain resilient, heal and create positive changes.

Often, it's when my clients are willing to pause, look at themselves honestly and gently and have the courage to be vulnerable and authentic that they are able to tune in to their needs, start the process of recovery and positive transformation and find true resilience.

The four attitudes for deep resilience practice

When I was a little girl, I spent a lot of time with my Uncle Geoff on his big property in rural New South Wales. He taught me to feed the animals, how to ride horses and grow food. He was a kind and wise man who had a huge positive impact on my life.

One of my favourite things was watching him break in horses. People would bring him their wild, rowdy and even sometimes dangerous horses and he would return them rideable (even by small kids) or able to pull a cart or wagon, and enjoying a close bond with humans.

How he did this would baffle people. He certainly had an unusual talent for it, but I knew some of his secrets from watching him at work. The greatest of these was his attitude towards the horses. He always treated them with kindness, respect, dignity and patience, and with a sprinkling of playfulness and humour thrown in too.

He would take his time to get to know and understand each horse and he didn't rush the process. He would observe the animal with interest for a while, coming closer to the horse, allowing it to get to know him and building up a sense of mutual trust and respect. He was never forceful or harsh. He was always kind. He believed in every horse's potential, and with repetition, patience and care, he trained them to do incredible things, way beyond what people thought possible.

Like Uncle Geoff, if we can bring helpful attitudes into the way we understand, relate to and interact with our mind, we can develop a more harmonious, friendly and respectful relationship with it, befriending and partnering with it rather than making it an enemy. If we can embody the four attitudes of deep resilience training, we can unlock the best in our own potential. These are: kindness, playful curiosity, patience and grit.

Kindness

It's important to be compassionate and understanding towards our mind, training it with kindness as you would if you were teaching a child to ride a bike. We are not trying to destroy the ego or suppress the mind but working to become a friendly ally. With kindness comes respect. Your mind is incredible and has kept you alive and safe as best as it could. It's been working hard for you so try creating a great partnership rather than being adversarial in any way.

Being harsh, mean or looking on your mind as an enemy only sets you up for more inner tension. Your mind, like all living things, will be more responsive if treated with love and understanding. We sometimes think being harsh with ourselves is a great way to learn but in fact the research shows that self-compassion is a much more effective and adaptive way forward.[18]

Playful curiosity

As much as possible, bring an attitude of lightness, humour and creativity to the process of working with and training your mind.

Playfulness encourages the mind to soften some of its survival-based tendencies, to be creative, flexible and open. Sometimes this means letting go of our preconceived ideas about being 'mature', 'grown up' or 'having it together' and instead allowing ourselves to access our childlike side where we are willing to see things with fresh eyes, try new things and play around, explore and experiment a bit.

At the start of every retreat I run, I encourage people to think of themselves as explorers. Let your life be a laboratory where you feel free to experiment, try new things, watch the results and see what insights, possibilities and experiences might emerge. Feel free to explore, challenge old ways of doing things, try on new ways of being, consider unusual approaches and interesting angles, challenge the status quo, test and refine possible approaches, free of expectation or judgement. If you do this, you might discover hidden depths, dimensions and skills that were always hiding inside you but have been previously overlooked.

Patience

When we are practising becoming deeply resilient, we need to be patient. We cannot force habits to change, or control how fast our wounds will heal or when insights and breakthroughs will come. All we can do is keep creating the conditions for these things to unfold and then allow the passing of time to grow the seeds of change in our lives.

Many of us live our lives pushing for a particular outcome and focused on getting results quickly, but when it comes to growing inner strength, this can be counterproductive. The more we try to force change, the less present, calm and at ease we are in each moment. It's a bit of a paradox but the more patient we are with ourselves, the more we set up the right conditions for positive change to unfold.

Grit

Also known as tenacity or determination, this is the quality of persisting at something you feel passionate about, sticking with it when you face obstacles. It is the ability to keep moving towards long-term meaningful goals and not be deterred even when things get tough.

When you have grit you stay committed to a task that may be boring, uncomfortable or arduous at times. It's about having a clear direction and the commitment to see it through.

Grit is the attitude required by an athlete who is training for a competition. They don't only practise when they feel like it, when the weather is nice, when they're in a good mood, when there is nothing more fun to do or when there's time to fit it in. The athlete trains regularly, every day, come rain, hail or shine and whether they feel like it or not. That's the attitude we need to create meaningful transformation in our selves and our lives. That's how we get the results we need and reap all the benefits that deep resilience has to offer.

Summary

In this chapter, we've learned about the nature of the human mind and how our primal survival-based programming can draw us into getting stuck in unhelpful thinking patterns like the negativity bias, hypervigilance and overthinking. We've introduced the first step in the RISE method, which comprises strategies for regulating your thoughts and emotions so that you can make your mind an asset and your ally, rather than fighting against it.

The key to successfully navigating hard times and maintaining resilience and wellbeing isn't pushing difficult thoughts away, ignoring them, stuffing them down, pretending everything is OK or covering them up with positive thinking. Instead, it's about developing skills to meet those thoughts in new, helpful and healthy ways.

We've learned about the four attitudes you need to cultivate for deep resilience; this is an important foundation. Beyond this, there are evidence-based skills – defusion, self-compassion and redirection – that work and form part of Step 1: Recognise and Regulate; you will learn more about them in the next chapters.

3
Follow The Golden Law

One of the most deeply transformative experiences of my own life happened around the age of eighteen. I was nursing a broken heart after a breakup. I remember walking through the neighbourhood near my house right after I'd had the conversation that ended the relationship; I was hurting so badly. I'd never had my heart broken before and it was such a deep, searing emotional pain. As I was walking, I was doing what I often did in those days when stressed: beating myself up mentally. Putting myself down, doubting myself and feeling angry at myself for being such a mess in that moment.

But then I stopped in the middle of the path and decided to apply something I had been learning on a course I had been attending. I said to myself in a soft compassionate voice, *This hurts. This is really hard.*

Then I put my hand on my heart as a gesture of kindness towards myself, and said mentally, *May I be kind to myself in this moment.* Tears started to roll softly down my cheeks. The tension in my body loosened and I let out a big sigh. I remember feeling so much genuine care towards myself.

I also set an intention to help myself through this pain as best I could. I clearly remember how this attitude shift made me feel so soothed, so centred and so grounded in that moment. It allowed me to also feel reassured that life would go on and that I would be OK. I had more of a sense of safety and calm within all the pain. I truly had my own back, for one of the first times in my life, and I remember making a silent commitment that I would look after myself, heal myself and support myself and go on to enjoy my life as best I could and find happiness, love and wellbeing.

I noticed how the storm of mental and emotional tension and turmoil that had always erupted when I was harsh and mean towards myself began to subside, and I felt a greater steadiness of mind and heart. I felt more in control, more empowered.

My path of developing inner strength had started a couple of years prior to this, with learning self-compassion. It came from the simple desire to alleviate my suffering and to be able to flourish, find peace and feel fulfilment. It was self-compassion that gave me the original motivation and drive to heal my mind, and find inner strength, but it had happened organically, and I didn't truly understand it for what it was. However, on this day, when I was heartbroken, a penny dropped. I knew I had an inner strength I could now draw on in a concrete way to support myself in the hard moments of my life, to help me overcome unhelpful habits, to grow healthier and stronger. Self-compassion, over time, totally revolutionised the way I treated myself and allowed me to heal the things inside me I had thought to be broken. It made me a happier person and gave me more grit; it allowed me to overcome self-doubt and keep moving towards the goals I had set for myself.

In my work with people over the years, I have seen that self-compassion is the foundation we need to build upon in order to become deeply resilient. Compassion for yourself is fundamental because if you don't have an attitude of respect and care towards yourself and a natural desire to support yourself and alleviate your suffering then it's hard to make any kind of effort to become stronger.

The golden law

We are often a good friend to others – thoughtful, considerate and kind – but what kind of friend are you to yourself? What impacts does that have on your quality of life – on the way you feel, the way your treat yourself, the way you allow yourself to be treated by others?

The golden law, or what is sometimes known as the golden rule, is a principle that appears through-out our ancient and modern history, from Ancient

Greece and the Persian Empire to eastern and western spiritual traditions, and it is also central to modern wisdom teachings. The law is simple: treat others as one would want to be treated by them. What we often don't realise is that this law also applies to ourselves. We should treat ourselves the way we would like to be treated by others – with kindness, respect, understanding and patience.

For most of us, the things that we crave the most when things get tough, are comfort, kindness, understanding and support from the people closest to us. But instead of treating ourselves that way, our minds often rub salt on our wounds. That harsh inner voice I mentioned earlier may tell us to toughen up, get over it and push through when what we actually need is rest and support. The mind might tell us we're weak or flawed for struggling in a hard time or feeling the way we do. It may criticise us, put us down or blame us for what is happening.

This harsh attitude towards ourselves creates a lot of extra tension, anxiety and heartache. In fact, these self-critical thoughts and behaviours can trigger our body's fight or flight system because they ramp up stress.

Imagine living in a house with someone who was constantly following you around criticising and judging you, telling you you're not good enough and that you have to be better. You could expect the energy to become quite tense, uneasy and demoralising. Now imagine having to live in that house when you're already going through a hard time. It would be truly debilitating.

You could say that our true home is our mind because although we can leave our houses, we carry our minds with us wherever we go.

Harsh thought processes, like the critical inner voice, diminish our motivation, resilience and initiative, whereas self-compassion and kindness increase them. When we speak to ourselves kindly, we bring soothing and calm to ourselves. Self-compassion can trigger our body's parasympathetic or 'soothing' system, and it even releases a powerful squirt of oxytocin, the 'love hormone', which reduces cortisol and calms cardiovascular stress.

Self-compassion is a skill that people sometimes initially have resistance to developing because they consider it to be soft, self-indulgent or think that it will make them lazy and irresponsible. They worry that they will lose their 'edge', or it will undermine their motivation and their ability to stay strong and be a support to others.

But research indicates that the opposite is true. Higher levels of self-compassion are linked to increased happiness, resilience and optimism; improved motivation and productivity; and a greater ability to bounce back after adversity and setbacks. It has also been shown to decrease anxiety, depression, rumination and fear of failure. Additionally, because self-compassionate people do not berate themselves when they fail, they are more able to admit mistakes, modify unhelpful behaviours, overcome obstacles and reach their goals.

To continue the analogy I used above, imagine your mind could become like a loving and supportive housemate. Someone who speaks to you with respect and kindness, encourages and coaches you when you're trying to reach big goals or overcome obstacles, who is always there for you when you are down. Your mind becomes a place where you feel safe and loved, where you can heal, gather strength, grow stronger and find inspiration and encouragement. It's a place where you can thrive.

This is the kind of drastic change that can happen in the mind when we practise self-compassion, and never is this more important than when we are facing a big challenge or experiencing difficulty in our lives.

What this all boils down to is that if we can learn to treat ourselves with greater kindness, we're going to be much better at handling our pain and stress, and we will bounce back faster too. Not only that, but because self-compassion makes us stronger, we're better able to support others around us too.

Make no mistake, self-compassion isn't a 'soft skill', a 'hippy thing', a sign of weakness or self-indulgence. Self-compassion is a valuable inner resource, the mother of all mental and emotional strengths. This is why we always start with following the golden law as our foundation.

Three reasons to practise self-compassion

First, without self-compassion our efforts to grow our inner strength can often be blocked. This is because without self-compassion we often get caught up in beliefs and behaviours that sabotage our ability to develop the strength we need or are looking for – beliefs like 'I'm broken,' 'I don't deserve to feel better,' 'I'm not lovable,' or 'I'm going to fail if I try that,' 'I'm not good enough,' or 'I'm just an idiot/failure/loser' can take over and subvert our attempts. Behaviours that drain, hurt and dismiss our long-term wellbeing, safety or true happiness can also dominate when we have little or no self-compassion in how we relate with ourselves.

Second, self-compassion motivates you to make positive changes in your life. Research indicates that self-compassion prompts us to take action to change unhelpful behaviours, look after our wellbeing and move towards meaningful goals.[19]

Research also shows that self-compassionate people have an orientation towards growth, persist longer in their efforts to change and are more likely to keep trying after setbacks.[20]

Through self-compassion, we make change; not because we feel unworthy and are pushing ourselves to be 'enough', but because we care about ourselves and want to be happy.

Third, being kind to yourself is good for others. When people are kind to themselves, they generally become more understanding, patient, tolerant and kinder to others. Think about times when you have been stressed or full of inner turmoil and how that affected the way you were able to show up in relationships. For most of us, we are less tolerant, more reactive, more impatient and not exactly the kindest version of ourselves. Consider how being kind to yourself may ripple out and touch the lives of your loved ones, co-workers, community and the wider world.

What is self-compassion?

There are a few different definitions of self-compassion but in essence it's about giving ourselves the same kindness and support we'd give to a dear friend.

When it comes to how we want to speak to ourselves in hard times, think of it like doing an inner U-turn. That compassion you naturally give to others when they're down – point it back at yourself. The invitation is to deliberately switch up your attitude towards yourself and the way you speak to yourself, to a more supportive and helpful tone.

Instead of judging yourself, putting yourself down, or berating yourself when you make a mistake, ignoring your pain with a 'get over it' or 'toughen up' mentality, or getting overtaken and overwhelmed by negative thoughts and emotions, stop to first acknowledge your pain by saying something to yourself mentally, like:

- *This hurts.*

- *This is really hard right now.*

- *Today was really tough.*

- *This is a moment of suffering.*

- *This is painful.*

Then offer yourself some words of kindness, encouragement and support. Think about what a supportive friend would say, and say it to yourself. For example:

- *I'm here for you.*

- *I'm sorry that you have to go through this.*

- *May I be kind to myself in this moment.*

- *Everyone makes mistakes sometimes. You're human.*

- *It's natural to feel this way. Everyone hurts sometimes.*

- *I've got your back. You're not alone.*

- *What can I do to support myself through this?*

- *What do I need right now, to help me through?*

Each time you catch your mind being harsh, critical or judgemental, do a U-turn and actively switch your inner tone, language, dialogue and attitude to be more compassionate. As best you can, follow the golden law all the way through your deep resilience journey.

EXERCISE 1: Two-minute exercise: Self-compassion practice

I invite you now to find a comfortable position – if possible, sitting upright rather than slouching – and just take a few moments to notice if you have any tension in your body. See if you can relax any tension a little. Let your jaw soften, the shoulders relax and the hands let go of any gripping.

Now bring to mind any situation that you're going through at the moment that's difficult. Take a few moments to really allow yourself to reflect on what's been happening in your life.

Notice any thoughts and feelings that arise in response to bringing this to mind.

Then, using a caring, warm and soft tone to your inner voice, begin by genuinely acknowledging the pain or stress that you have been feeling and offer yourself some compassion. If you can't think of the right words, try saying to yourself:

This is really hard. May I be kind to myself in this moment.

And take a moment to absorb those words.

What did you notice in trying this out? The majority of people I work with find that in offering some compassionate words to themselves they feel a degree of instant relief, inner calm or soothing. This kind of caring self-talk helps them to feel a bit better, quickly. However, for some people, when they practise self-compassion, it can initially make things feel a bit worse as it can trigger a whole bunch of negative self-talk and difficult feelings. Don't worry if you are in the latter category because, as we journey through this book and you continue to integrate these skills, you will find this easier and feel more soothing and confidence.

You can access a guided audio version of this meditation (as well as all the other meditations in this book and some additional resources) at www.melliobrien.com/bookgifts

Compassionate actions

It's not just kind words but also kind actions that can make all the difference in tough times. As you can see, some of the cues above are intended to inquire into actions you can take to actively support, nourish and care for yourself.

Compassionate or nourishing actions might be things like taking the extra rest you need, having a warm bath, calling a friend, working with a therapist or coach, eating a healthy meal, going for walks and doing hobbies that nourish you and lift your spirits. It's just about taking small actions, step by step, that move us towards greater ease, wellbeing and agency.

This might also involve reducing draining activities or actions. Draining actions you may choose to limit or cut out during hard times might be eating junk food, scrolling on your phone, overworking, spending too much time alone, drinking alcohol, hanging out in certain environments. It could take the form of setting boundaries with people, saying no to certain things, or saying yes to others.

Taking baby steps when changing habits is perfectly fine and, in itself, can be an act of compassion. Small changes, little by little, made with an attitude of care and thoughtfulness of your own wellbeing, that feel achievable, nourishing and not too overwhelming, can be a great place to start. Remember to be kind to yourself and, if you fall into old habits, remind yourself that the process of change can be tricky and often takes time. Offer yourself a few words of kindness and remain focused on the path of making positive changes to improve things for yourself, at a pace that feels supportive for you.

EXERCISE 2: A simple self-care plan

Something I often do when I am working with clients is make a simple self-care plan to support the rest of the deep resilience journey. We can do this in two steps. First, get a sheet of paper and draw a line down the centre. Then on one side write down things that you do in the flow of your daily life (or used to do that you enjoy) that are nourishing. Examples might include sitting in the sun with a tea, a sport you like, time spent with family, quiet time to rest, walking in nature, a healthy meal. All the things that give you energy and restore your vitality.

Next, write a list of things you do that drain you and that you could reduce or cut out in tough times. Some examples of draining actions might be eating junk food, scrolling on the phone, overworking, spending too much time alone, drugs, alcohol, hanging out in certain environments that are not helpful. These are things that reduce your energy, deplete you or lower your wellbeing, vitality, mood or ability to be present.

The second step is to create your 'three fundamentals to thrive' list. Use your nourishing and draining lists as inspiration to figure out your three fundamentals, the most important things that you can do, ongoing, to support your journey ahead.

Your fundamentals to thrive are three actions that, when engaged in regularly, act as a support system to help us stay stronger, more energised and promote healing, resilience and wellbeing in tricky times.

When identifying your own three fundamentals to thrive for your self-care plan, try to make them as simple and achievable as possible. It should feel nourishing and supportive to put this plan into action, not difficult or overwhelming.

Examples might be ensuring that you go for a walk a set number of times per week, committing to eating a certain amount of healthy food each week, scheduling a regular catch up or call with a friend, speaking to a therapist or other form of healing support regularly, making time for a hobby you love, reducing your work hours a bit or saying no to events or things that drain you and yes to those you find nourishing.

Summary

Of all the inner strengths we can develop, self-compassion is one of the most fundamental. We learn many different kinds of skills in this life: how to drive a car, how to type on a computer and so on. But very few of us in this modern world are encouraged to take the time to learn the skills that give us robust inner strength and support our happiness. By learning to practise self-compassion we totally transform our basic way of relating to ourselves. This lays the groundwork for giving us the grit, the flexibility and the motivation to keep growing and hardwiring our psychological and spiritual resources, until eventually we are able to hardwire in deep resilience as a way of being and it starts to become second nature.

In the rest of this book, we are embarking on a journey towards becoming deeply resilient. On this journey, the best companion you could possibly have is self-compassion.

4
Defusion

In this chapter, we'll explore the idea of thought fusion – and defusion. As we've learned, the mind continually makes up stories and meanings with the pulling power of a Hollywood blockbuster. We can't help but have thoughts – it's a natural part of having a mind with survival-based conditioning – but that's OK because the thoughts themselves are not a problem for us and cause us no distress unless we become *fused* with them.

Have you ever wondered:

- *Why do I keep rehashing painful or embarrassing memories?*

- *Why can't I stop worrying and overthinking, then becoming stressed and anxious, when I know it's not helpful?*

- *Why am I so hard on myself when deep down I know this is not all my fault?*

- *Why can't I stop thinking so negatively about myself and others in this situation?*

- *Why am I engulfed by self-doubt and fear when I attempt to step out of my comfort zone or take a risk?*

- *Why do I care and worry so much about what other people think of me?*

- *Why am I continuously comparing myself to others, always feeling like I'm falling short?*

- *Why do I never feel enough or content with what I already have? Why am I always wanting more?*

- *Why can't I find inner peace and happiness?*

Many of my clients ask themselves these same questions, which all share a common root: they come about when we're stuck in FEAR, and specifically when we're fused with unhelpful thoughts. The term 'cognitive fusion' was coined by Dr Steven Hayes, who developed acceptance and commitment therapy. When we're experiencing cognitive fusion, we can't separate ourselves from our thoughts. We mistake our thoughts for reality. We become caught up in our thoughts, which in turn means we become more emotionally reactive to them. We can even feel 'caught in our heads' and therefore more disconnected or distant from the world and even the people around us.

The opposite of cognitive fusion is cognitive defusion.[21] Cognitive defusion involves taking a step back from what's going on in our minds and detaching a little from our thoughts. In this state of defusion, we can observe our thoughts and other internal processes without getting lost in them, stuck in them or fused with them. We can simply notice our thoughts, watch them, accept them and let them go, if we choose to.

The Deep Resilience Method, in alignment with the research by Wegner mentioned earlier, asserts that thoughts themselves are not inherently problematic, regardless of their content. Instead, it's our relationship with the thoughts that matters.

Rather than suppressing, avoiding or being taken over by thoughts, the Deep Resilience Method offers a more adaptive response: we consciously change our relationship with thoughts and develop a more compassionate, understanding, wise and skilful relationship with our mind, instead of fighting it, struggling against it or succumbing to it.

Fusion with thoughts

When we become fused with our thoughts, we get caught up in them to such an extent that they exert a heavy influence over our emotions, behaviour and perceptions. We become dominated by them, which greatly hinders our mental and emotional flexibility and strength.

In a state of fusion, we mistake our thoughts for reality. That is, we buy into them, we take them seriously and tend to believe them unquestioningly. Our behaviour is then governed by our thoughts as we obey them, play them out and act impulsively in response to them. Our sense of self also gets entangled with these thoughts, and we find it hard to know our self beyond them, which can stifle our potential, block our access to wholeness and keep us stuck in ways of thinking and living that aren't truly serving us. In fusion, we become emotionally reactive to our thoughts; we get thrown around and dragged down by them.

In this state, we don't have much choice in how we react; it just happens automatically, and it can be hard to make a change.

Thought defusion

When we defuse from thoughts, our relationship with them is completely transformed. No longer stuck in or entangled with our thoughts, we can let go of them as needed, open up mental space and see them from a new vantage point – looking *at* the thoughts rather than looking *from* them.

Once defused, we can clearly see the difference between a thought and reality. We understand that thoughts are just mental events, bits of language that move through our heads and not 'the truth' – so we don't automatically believe or buy into all of our thoughts. We only give them our attention and follow them if they are valuable or helpful.

Since we have more mental space, we have the power to choose our response to thoughts. This gives us new power, freedom and flexibility. We do not play our thoughts out reactively. We can question and assess them for their validity and usefulness and work with them, as needed, in ways that empower, uplift and support us.

We also understand that our self and our thoughts about ourselves are distinct, totally different things. You are not your thoughts, and this is seen clearly. Who you are – your depth, your wholeness – is something much deeper, greater and more multifaceted, something that can't be reduced down to a handful of judgements and thoughts. When you see past your thoughts about yourself, who you really are can be known, felt and will shine through in a more authentic and fulfilling way.

Like breaking a spell, defusion releases us from the grip of thoughts and, subsequently, their influence over the way we feel, act and see the world and ourselves. We are no longer thrown around by them, pulled into suffering and stress.

More freedom and peace of mind emerge, along with an ability to access the deeper resources, strengths and potentials within us. Defusion techniques are powerful enough to handle even the darkest, scariest and most intimidating thoughts.

Let's unpack a simple example of defusion to demonstrate the concept. Imagine waking up one morning in bed and you look out the window to see that it's raining. In that moment, the mind might say, *Urgghhh, what a dreadful day!*

Is it true that the day is dreadful? Of course not – it's simply raining. However, if you believe that thought – that is, you become fused with it – then you will mistake the thought for reality. You unquestioningly believe that it is a dreadful day and there is no space within you to be able to consider an alternative view. Now that you have bought into that story in your mind, you become emotionally reactive to it. You might begin to feel sad, bitter or grumpy and you could also start to play out that emotion: your body slumps, a frown appears on your face, you become impatient with other people and the traffic, and you're irritable all day at work. You don't notice the smiles from strangers, the pleasant taste of your coffee or the beauty of your garden. You end up having a dreadful day because you believed the thought that told you it was one.

Now rewind the scene. Here's what it looks like with defusion.

The same morning, same bed, same weather, same moment. Again, the thought arises, *Oh, what a dreadful day!* This time, however, you simply notice the thought arise and then dissolve. You don't believe it or take it seriously as there's no need to: after all, it's just some sounds, bits of language that pass through your mind. You have noticed the thought as a mental event, but you don't get hooked by it, so it passes quickly, as thoughts do when we don't attach to them. You're left free to lay there all cosy in your bed, looking out of the window, feeling relaxed and enjoying the rain. Your day goes on, unaffected by what was nothing more than fleeting sounds and words in the mind – no more, no less.

It may seem like a bit of a paradox, but one of the most effective things you can do with an unwanted or unpleasant thought is to acknowledge it and then allow it. This gives you the ability to defuse from it. This process of looking at the thought (recognising it) creates some mental distance between you and it so that you can see it for what it is – a brief mental event, a snippet of sound, a collection of words inside your head that are moving through your awareness, something that arises, unfolds and then passes. If we can recognise a thought in this way, we disarm it, we realise it is not as powerful or scary as it once seemed and it loses its power. Instead of running from or fighting the white bear in your mind, you can let it naturally walk by – appearing and then passing, as all thoughts do.

This is the process of defusion.

EXERCISE 3: One-minute exercise: What is a thought?

Take a moment to think about something you're planning to do later on today or tomorrow.

Focus on examining the thoughts as they arise. What is a thought anyway?

With an attitude of curiosity, notice what form the thoughts take, how long they stay around, what they're made of. Try to be curious, not about the content of the thought but about what a thought *is*. Closing your eyes now, try this for around a minute.

What did you notice? You might discover that one part of you is thinking while another part is observing that thinking. There are your thoughts – and there's you, observing them. The observer is not affected by the thoughts and is able to let them arise and pass.

Another observation you may have had is that thoughts are not as solid and fixed as they sometimes seem – that they are mental events. They are ephemeral; they arise and disappear quickly and are quite fleeting.

You can access a guided audio version of this meditation as well as all the other meditations in this book (and a suite of five other free gifts) at www.melliobrien.com/bookgifts

---

Untangling suffering from pain

In my work with clients over the years, I have come to see that the 'Aha! moment' for many, in regard to the recognising and regulating step, comes when they can clearly make the distinction between pain and suffering.

In any given moment of our lives, there are two basic dimensions to our experience: primary and secondary. Primary experience involves our direct experience of the present moment, our sense perceptions – what we can feel, see, hear, taste and smell. Some sense perceptions are pleasant or pleasurable, others are unpleasant or painful. Secondary experience is the thoughts we have *about* our primary experience – all the meanings, stories and judgements we make in our minds.

Let's say you're sitting in a car in a traffic jam. Your primary experience is the feeling of your hands on the wheel and your feet on the pedals, the sight of the cars that are stopped in front of you and the trees and buildings around you, the smell of flowers blooming on the side of the road and the exhaust from other cars in front, behind and beside you, and the sound of the music playing from the car radio.

In that situation, what kinds of thoughts might arise? Maybe things like *Oh my god, this is so annoying. I hate traffic jams. This is horrible. I'm such an idiot, why did I come this way? I can't believe this. These other drivers are so incompetent. They need to go back to driving school!* These thoughts are your secondary experience and when we think these kinds of thoughts, we start to become stressed, irritated, anxious and grumpy – all forms of psychological suffering.

Sometimes unpleasant or painful things happen to us in our primary experience, including traffic jams. We can't avoid that, but the psychological suffering that is created by our unhelpful thoughts at the level of secondary experience? That's completely optional, as Viktor Frankl, the American psychiatrist and Holocaust survivor, observed: 'Between stimulus and response there is a space. In that space is our power to choose our response. In our response lies our growth and our freedom.'[22] We do have a choice to massively reduce, or even completely end, our psychological suffering.

Pain is all the unpleasant and unwanted things that happen in our primary experience, much of which we have no control over: sickness, ageing, loss, heartbreak, misfortune, the noisy neighbour who plays loud music all night while we're trying to sleep, traffic jams, missed planes, the cat pee on the brand-new couch (it was never the same again...) and so on.

Suffering arises in secondary experience. It's the inner tension, resistance and turmoil created by our thoughts about what is happening in our lives: sulking because I have the flu, hating my wrinkles, complaining incessantly about the noise my neighbour made and how tired I am all the next day, shooting death stares at other drivers in the traffic while I mutter to myself about their incompetence, moaning that the new plane ticket will cost me twice as much or lamenting that my couch is now ruined and I'll never be able to find another one at that price again. That's suffering.

Suffering can take many forms, including frustration, annoyance, insecurity, resentment and low mood to anxiety, rage, fear, depression, helplessness and despair. On a rational level, of course I know we all age and part of ageing is getting wrinkles. I know we all get sick sometimes, people will do things I don't like or want, and trains will run late. I know that life won't always go my way. In practice and in lived experience, however, it's a different story because suffering – the psychological tension and turmoil around pain – arises unconsciously and almost automatically. Our mind's knee-jerk reactive response to any painful or unwanted sensation or event is, unfortunately, to pile dense layers of suffering on top of it. Going through heartbreak, loss, uncertainty and misfortune is already hard enough, so what we don't want to do is cause ourselves even more suffering in an already painful time. Fortunately, once you learn the skills to let go of suffering, you can use your inner resources to deal with the pain.

EXERCISE 4: Three-minute exercise: Pain vs suffering – recognising the source of the struggle

Start by drawing two boxes on a piece of paper or in a notebook. In the first box, write down your situation, the source of your pain – for example, 'I lost my job'/'my partner left me'/'I have been diagnosed with an illness'/'my neighbours are playing music loudly all night'/'I'm struggling with an addiction'.

Now consider the situation you have described, and in the second box, note down any thoughts you have that create additional suffering. These could be thoughts that amplify stress, make you feel insecure, small or anxious, limit your potential and hold you back, increase anger and hostility or cause you to feel helpless or disempowered.

Once you can more clearly identify and be aware of some of the thoughts creating suffering can you begin to challenge them and change them (which we will explore in the next chapter).

Summary

In this chapter, we have seen how we can easily get hooked (fused) into ways of thinking that don't help us and which can cause a lot of suffering and disempowerment on top of an already difficult time. Learning to recognise our unhelpful mental patterns is a groundbreaking step to finding our deepest resilience.

We have also introduced the concept of defusion as a solution to overcome suffering and better deal with the difficulty and pain we might be facing. Defusion sets the stage for us to learn how to regulate our thoughts in ways that empower, uplift and give us back a sense of control.

5
Stay Above The Line

We all know the incredible power of the mind. With it we can create, but we can also destroy. Our thoughts hold an unseen power that is often the root cause of a great deal of our distress and dismay. However, now that we can more clearly recognise the patterns creating our suffering, and we understand the importance of defusion, we can learn how to use defusion to break free of the patterns that harm, disempower and hinder us and shift the mind towards new patterns that free, uplift, empower and heal us.

Sometimes just the simple act of recognising our thoughts for what they are can be enough to create that necessary distance for defusion to take place. As we learned in the previous chapter, once we look directly at the thought and see it for what it is, it loses its hold over us and its power dissipates, like breaking a spell. The suffering associated with that thought then naturally dissipates and we regain greater freedom and peace of mind.

However, there are times when our thoughts can be particularly charged, frantic, racing or agitated. These thoughts can be 'sticky' to work with, which means we have to take extra steps to defuse from them and reclaim our point of power and our ability to respond. Luckily, we have a simple way to disentangle from our racing, scary or unhelpful thoughts, calm our minds, come into inner balance and think more clearly.

It starts with a simple tool called the mental strength line.

The mental strength line

A favourite tool of my clients, one that many report finding particularly useful in identifying when they are caught in unhelpful thinking patterns, is also one of the simplest. In fact, it's nothing more than a simple black line – the mental strength line.

If you are above the line, you are in your strength. That is, you are defused from unhelpful thoughts and relating to what is happening in a helpful, nourishing or empowering way. A way that eases rather that increases suffering. Below the line? You're fused with unhelpful thinking styles that generate suffering of one kind or another.

How do you use the mental strength line? It works like this. Ask yourself this simple question about the thoughts in your mind as you go about your daily life: *Right now, am I below the line or above the line?*

How do you know? You are below the line if you are fused with unhelpful thoughts – that is, ones that cause you some form of psychological suffering.

Above the line: Defused and able to respond	= Strength
Below the line: Fused with unhelpful thoughts and reactive	= Suffering

Unhelpful thoughts include not only those that ramp up stress, anguish, anxiety and insecurity but also thoughts that are disempowering, limit our potential or pull us into pessimism, resentment and hostility. Remember there is a difference between pain and suffering. We do not have control over all of our circumstances. Sometimes painful, unpleasant and unwanted things will happen. However, we do have the power to choose to let go of suffering and shift back into a more helpful response in any given moment. Understanding the mental strength line is the first step to help you do that.

You can use the mental strength line at any time, but it's especially important when you feel stressed, resentful, insecure, reactive, anxious, overwhelmed or are in a low mood. Take a moment to check in, with an attitude of curiosity and compassion, to see what the source of the struggle is and find out if it's your thoughts that are causing some of your distress, suffering and struggle.

Remember, it's not a problem if you're having unhelpful thoughts. It's only a problem if you're *fused* with those thoughts. The problem is, we often don't notice when we are fused with unhelpful thinking patterns until they have already dragged us down, pulled us into emotional reactivity and held us back, and we become stuck in a rut.

This line is a recognition tool – an invitation to investigate your thoughts, gain insight and maintain self-awareness. It takes just a moment to stop and ask yourself, *Where am I at this moment, above the line or below the line? Is my way of thinking helpful or unhelpful? Am I in suffering or in my strength?* By doing this, you will become really good at recognising unhelpful thought patterns and creating the mental space to let them go.

Being below the line isn't 'bad', 'wrong' or a sign of failure (if those kinds of self-judging thoughts arise, simply notice that they are not helpful). It's just a sign that you have a normal human mind like the rest of us. Recognising that you're below the line is not a cause for self-judgement; it's a moment of awakening, a moment of choice, a moment of success, a moment of power.

When we can recognise that we are below the line, we can choose to let go of suffering and the thoughts that make life harder and instead choose strength. We can do this as an act of wisdom, kindness and self-care. After all, if you're already going through a hard time, the last thing you need is to add more suffering and distress. By shifting back above the line, you will become more balanced, clear-headed and empowered, and you stay connected to your inner resources to help you deal with the challenges.

Having an influx of painful feelings and negative thoughts is a natural response to hard times. Our goal is not to get rid of them but to change our relationship with them. We're learning to notice what is working for us and what isn't, what helps and what harms, what sets us free and what holds us back.

If you find yourself below the line – that is, you recognise that you have been hooked by an unhelpful thought – then your next step is to regulate it and shift back into your strength. Let's introduce a powerful tool that can help you do just that.

Name It, Tame It, Reframe It: A simple three-step defusion technique

This practice blends three powerful evidence-based defusion skills into one simple on-the-go technique. It is designed to give you the ability to defuse from unhelpful below-the-line thoughts that cause suffering, disempowerment and stress, and redirect your mental focus in helpful and skilful ways as needed.

These three skills can all be used as standalone tools that you can use at any time and often, the first two steps will be enough for you to be fully defused and back in your strength. Thoughts can no longer dominate, take over and cause suffering once you are sufficiently defused. Sometimes, however, we may need or want to use the additional step of 'reframe it' to practise shifting our mental focus in a more helpful, uplifting and empowering direction so that we can stand firm in our position above the line and harness the power of our minds to unlock our inner resources and take more life-affirming and positive steps forward. Combined, the three steps become a robust and effective way to regulate thoughts effectively.

Step 1: Name It

The first step is a variation of a long-used defusion technique called mental naming or labelling. Commonly used in meditation to unhook from thoughts and feelings, it can also be a powerful tool in daily life. It's a way of turning towards and directly acknowledging a thought. Often, mental naming is as simple as saying to yourself mentally, *Just thinking*, as soon as you notice yourself getting caught up in a thought.

Learn to thank the mind, rather than fight the mind

My favourite mental noting practice is inspired by the work of Dr Russ Harris (a renowned Acceptance and Commitment Therapy practitioner). In his book *The Happiness Trap*,[23] he describes a form of mental noting called 'thanking your mind'. I have used a variation of this for many years in my work with clients and found it to be incredibly helpful to allow people to shift gears quickly and efficiently as a first step of this process of defusion. Here's how to use it:

As soon as you notice a thought has pulled you below the line, you say to yourself mentally, *Thanks, Mind, but that's not very helpful.*

Why the thank you? The reason I like to use this kind of naming is because we're doing two things when we thank the mind. We are recognising the thought, but in the way I use it, we are also reminding ourselves to relate to the thought in a helpful and skilful way. Thanking the mind is a way of acknowledging that although it's not a helpful thought, everything your mind is doing is an attempt to protect and serve you. It is not your enemy and it's not out to get you or trying to hurt you. Your mind is like a faithful guard dog trying to keep you safe. It simply doesn't know any better than to play out its inherited and conditioned patterns. It's a bit stuck in the past and needs you to train, guide and soothe it. Thanking the mind is like patting your inner guard dog, letting it know you heard it, it's done its job and can relax now.

Thanking the mind is important because we don't want to get locked into a hostile, tense or adversarial relationship with our mind, to be at war with ourselves. This only intensifies the sense of inner struggle and can deepen fusion with thoughts over time. By first thanking the mind, we not only defuse from the thought, we simultaneously meet it with understanding, respect, gentleness and a greater awareness and appreciation of its role and function. It is a simple step with big implications and effects. It is the start of our journey to totally revolutionise our relationship with our mind and ourselves.

Now if your mind says, *You're an idiot! You'll never amount to anything*, you meet it with a wise inner smile and reply (in a friendly tone), *Thanks, Mind, but that's not very useful or helpful right now*.

If it says, *This shouldn't be happening. Why does everything bad always happen to me? What's wrong with me?* you kindly reply, *Thanks, Mind, but that's not useful or helpful, buddy*.

Even when the mind is at its nastiest, *I hate this stupid 'Thanking the mind' crap! Stop kidding yourself. You're never going to change. You're just a no-hoper. You've always been one, you'll always been one and you're too fat and you look horrible in that outfit!* You respond gently and with kindness, *Thanks, Mind, but that's not so helpful*.

No matter what the mind says to you, no matter how scary, dramatic, mean and horrible, you simply continue with that practice, perhaps even simplifying it down to an inner smile (a smile that knows your mind is just trying to help) and a friendly short reply, *Thanks, Mind*.

Mental naming or labelling of thoughts can significantly decrease the intensity of difficult emotions and stress. That's because naming creates distance between you and your thoughts, giving you space to realise that you don't need to believe everything your mind tells you, which in turn alleviates suffering.

This new way of relating to thoughts has been a total game changer for many of my clients. No longer locked in an unrelenting battle with themselves and their thoughts, many report an incredible sense of relief and inner stability.

It's important to again bring that attitude of self-compassion into this practice. Like a wise parent or elder, let your inner tone be infused with warmth and kindness as you 'name it'; humour and playfulness help, too. Having this attitude of love and light-heartedness goes a long way in allowing the mind to relax and settle. Feel free to play around with the wording, get creative with it and make it your own.

In summary, we don't need to try to fight the thoughts, change them or argue with the mind (*No, I am not a no-hoper! I'm great, shut up! I have all these great things about me*). We know the mind is just doing what it's designed to do and generating fear-based thoughts in an attempt to keep us safe. The mind has a sort of innocence about it. It's wired this way from evolution and is a bit like an outdated software program running in our heads. It's just trying to keep us safe but a lot of the time the patterns it runs to do this are simply not that useful or helpful for us in the moment, so we need to train it with patience, gentle persistence and understanding.

Mental labelling allows us to step back and unhook from a thought so it no longer has a grip on us. It gives us the space to make a choice about how we want to be in that moment, and now we can simply choose not to pile on more suffering, stress and hardship.

We do this as an act of care, compassion and wisdom towards ourselves and our mind.

Step 2: Tame It

In the second step, we use the practice of mindfulness to further defuse from thoughts and ground our attention back to our primary experience in the present moment, to our sense perceptions. We will be exploring mindfulness more deeply as part of the second step of the RISE framework (Inhabit the Present Moment), but we cannot recognise or regulate our thoughts (or indeed complete any other steps of the Deep Resilience Method) without mindfulness, so let's have a brief introduction.

Mindfulness is an ancient concept, with roots in a wide range of spiritual and religious traditions, including most martial arts, yoga, tai chi, nondualism, Buddhism, Taoism, Hinduism, Judaism and many others. Over the last thirty years, modern psychology has started to recognise the many benefits of mindfulness training and it has now become an empirically supported intervention.[24]

Mindfulness can be defined in a variety of ways, but they all share these three basic elements. The first is that mindfulness is a way of paying attention on purpose, or intentionally. A lot of the time, our attention is hooked by the mind and swept away by all kinds of thoughts, opinions and beliefs and may carry us to various places that we may or may not have wanted to go. The old software program in the mind is running on autopilot mode and we often don't realise it. Mindfulness involves noticing that our attention has been fused with thinking, and then choosing to take back control.

The second part is that, through mindfulness, we bring attention to the experience of the present moment. Note that mindfulness is a process of being *aware of* our present moment experience, not of *thinking about* it. We are immersing ourselves in the present without engaging in mentally evaluating it.

The third element is that we pay attention with a certain kind of attitude: with curiosity, kindness and acceptance. This includes accepting our thoughts and feelings (both positive and negative). Even if our experience is difficult, painful or unpleasant, we can be open to it and have a kind and curious attitude towards it, instead of running from or fighting with it.

With these three elements, mindfulness allows us to find a steady ground within ourselves and to gain flexibility of attention: the ability to consciously direct or focus attention on different aspects of experience. We can use mindfulness to step out of habitual, reactive patterns and instead intentionally choose both our response and where to direct our attention.

Mindfulness is usually taught via meditation. However, in the Deep Resilience Method, meditation is only one tool in our kit of mindfulness skills. In this book, you will learn many mindfulness-based skills, most of which are simple and can be learned in just a couple of minutes.

The power of awareness

A good analogy to understand mindfulness is to think of your mind as being like an ocean. Waves of thoughts and feelings are continually moving on the surface. Sometimes the ocean is calm, other times it's choppy and buffeted by winds and storms. If our attention gets stuck on the surface all the time, we are like a small raft, tossed around at the mercy of the waves of thoughts, conditioned patterns and feelings. If, however, we can learn to drop our attention a little deeper, we can take a step back from those thoughts and feelings and not get so thrown around by them. We become more like a large and powerful stream-lined yacht with a deep ballast and a high mast, carving through the waves gracefully, charting a steady course through the storms.

We also find that just as below the ocean's surface there is a calm, deep and still place, so it is with us. If we can shift our attention from being caught up in the surface waves of thoughts and feelings and instead anchor ourselves in a deeper awareness, we can find a place of calm, strength and wisdom. We can do that through the practice of grounding our attention back in the present moment. Being mindful.

Dropping into a deeper awareness through mindfulness gives us back our power. We untangle from the thoughts that create anxieties, insecurity, negativity and restless nights. It gives us the mental space and flexibility to choose to make a shift from below the mental strength line to above it, so we can then live more intentionally.

You will recall that we always have two levels of experience going on: primary (what you can see, hear, taste, touch and smell) and secondary (your thoughts about the primary experiences). If you are below the mental strength line, then you are caught up in that secondary experience and fused with your thoughts. This will amplify suffering, stress and struggle and draw you into reactivity.

You 'tame it' when you are able to use the practice of mindfulness to unhook from thinking by shifting your focus to the present moment and your primary experience, your sense perceptions. Mindful awareness connects you to the present moment and deepens your defusion from thoughts. Remember that you're not struggling with the thought itself. There's no need to push it away, stuff it down, pretend it's not there or disguise it with a positive costume. Let the thought be, and make your main focus connecting with your primary experience. The present moment is your point of power. Return to it whenever you get caught up.

There are a number of ways that you can connect with your senses in the moment:

- Focus on your breath and take three deep breaths.

- Feel your feet on the ground.

- Listen to the sounds of the present moment.

- Look around you and focus on one object in your view (such as a plant, picture, lamp or you could look out the window to a tree). Take it in for a couple of moments.

- Feel your hands. You can even give them a little squeeze.

- Deliberately let go of tension in the body – unclench the jaw, relax the shoulders...

- Wriggle your fingers and toes.

- Stretch your body and feel the sensation of the stretch in your body.

EXERCISE 5: Two-minute exercise: Practice to ground your attention

When you're ready, take a moment to shift your attention to the feeling of the breath moving in your body and specifically in your torso. Feel the sensations as your body gently swells and expands a little with each inhale and subsides with each exhale (you can place your hands on your belly or chest if that's helpful). Try to stay in touch with the feeling of the breath, letting your attention ride each wave of the breath from the beginning to the end.

As you do this, the mind may wander and you may find yourself thinking about problems, to-do lists, worries or even what's for dinner. No problem. Each time the mind wanders, practise grounding your attention back to your senses, say to yourself (with patience and warmth), *Thanks, Mind*, then come back to feeling the sensation of the breath. Repeat the process of grounding as many times as needed.

Try this for about a minute now, with eyes open or closed.

Then, with an attitude of curiosity, close your eyes and for around sixty seconds, tune in to all the sounds around you, listening to them as they arise and disappear like notes in a song. Each time the mind pulls you away into thinking, mentally say, *Thanks, Mind,* and then, gently and intentionally, invite it back to the sounds, grounding your attention back in the here and now, over and over again.

You can access a guided audio version of this meditation (as well as all the other meditations in this book and some additional resources) at www.melliobrien.com/bookgifts

---

What did you notice? People experience various things when they first try grounding attention in their primary experience. Some find it a bit tricky at first, but, with practice, most people discover that it helps them find an inner calm and stability, like finding a safe harbour in a storm.

Another observation you may have had is that tension in the body is often released when tension in the mind is released. As you switch into mindful awareness, the instinctive fight-or-flight response tends to calm down, so the body starts to relax and the mind begins to slow.

Don't worry if you didn't experience these things or found it hard. Rest assured that, like any skill, grounding your attention gets easier and more available to you with practice.

In many cases, this simple practice of grounding is all it takes to defuse from any unhelpful thoughts and therefore 'tame' them. Taming in the way I use the word here doesn't have anything to do with force, coercion or rough handling. We tame thoughts by simply unhooking ourselves and then the thoughts lose their hold over us.

The good news is, with these two simple steps, you'll often find you are sufficiently defused and so already back above the mental strength line. It's really that simple. Now you can set an intention to proceed with whatever you are doing, but with more awareness. I encourage you to do this each time you defuse, to take that mindful awareness with you into the next moments and activities of your day. That way, rather than acting from fusion with the thoughts in our heads, we can act with greater awareness and purpose, handle our challenges more effectively and feel calmer, clearer-headed and happier as we go about our day.

Often grounding is all you need to do to shift back above the mental strength line. Sometimes, however, we will need more, particularly when those thoughts are charged, loud or 'sticky' and it's difficult to find your centre again.

Then you might like to take the extra step of reframing your thoughts.

Step 3: Reframe it

As we know, the mind is a story-making machine that can be a powerful asset but also, at other times, our own worst enemy. In hard times, the mind tends to tip into FEAR-based patterns that make things harder.

As Wegner's research showed, as well as many other studies on effective thought regulation, trying to get rid of the white bear (unhelpful thoughts) doesn't work and in fact often makes things worse. More useful tools to support us in staying mentally strong as we navigate through hard times include what Wegner called redirection and I call reframing.

In times of challenge, pain and difficulty, working skilfully with our mind's story-making habit can be the difference between rising to our challenges and coming out the other side wiser and stronger, or feeling crushed or defeated by them and falling into despair, hopelessness or depression.

We have already learned with the first two steps (Name It and Tame It) how to defuse from unhelpful thoughts, which can be enough to shift back above the mental strength line, but sometimes we need a little bit more. Reframing is an especially helpful tool to shift your thinking in ways that allow creativity, flexibility and confidence, and that unlock your higher and deeper potentials.

Redirecting or reframing your mental focus is an effective way to regulate our thoughts and feel empowered and in control again. Reframing is essentially about changing the way something is perceived, understood, related to or described. In this step, we apply this idea to our internal dialogue.

There are two basic forms of reframing: changing focus and changing meaning. Both aim to shift your mental focus in a new, more helpful direction.

Change the focus

I remember when I was a teenager learning to drive, realising the importance of not focusing where you don't want the car to go. I learned quickly that if you look off to the side while you're driving then you tend to veer in that direction, so you have to keep your eyes exactly where you want to go, especially in an emergency situation. You don't look at the tree that you don't want to crash into, instead you look out to the open space where you *do* want the car to go.

While we can easily understand this principle in relation to driving, we overlook the same effect when it comes to our mental focus and end up focusing on things that take us into a mental-emotional state that we don't want to be in. We never want to choose to feel anxious, overwhelmed, hopeless or hateful, but we often focus on the things that take us there.

In any given moment, there are many different things we can focus on. Our attention is finite so there are only a limited number of things we can focus on at any given time. For instance, right now, you can focus on the feeling of the soles of your feet. Or you can pay attention to the sounds around you. When we turn our focus in one direction, other things fade into the background a little. That doesn't mean those other things disappear (we are still aware of sights and sensations in the background) but they are not taking up the majority of our attention. In this way, focus is like a spotlight on a stage that highlights and hones in on a certain aspect of our experience.

This is important to understand because what you focus on will change, often dramatically, how you feel and respond.

There are so many different things you can choose to focus on as you go about life. For instance you can focus on your partner's flaws, mistakes and weaknesses or you can focus on their strengths, good qualities and kind acts. Will this change how you feel (both in yourself and about them) and act towards them? You bet. In a difficult situation, you can focus on what possibilities, solutions and opportunities will get you through, or you can focus on what you hate about it, how unfair it is and how stressful it will be. Will that make a difference to how you handle the challenge? For sure.

In a crisis some people focus on who is to blame and get angry, and some focus on how they can help and become compassionate and brave. If you focus on the good in your life rather than what you lack, will this be the difference between feeling fulfilled and dissatisfied? It most likely will be. If you focus on what's 'wrong' with you versus what's right, could this be the difference between having the confidence to achieve your dreams or letting self-doubt and discouragement hold you back? In many cases, it is. Such is the power of focus.

There's a common saying, 'Where your focus goes, energy flows and what you focus on grows.' This phrase perfectly captures the power of consciously choosing where to direct your focus.

Your mental and emotional states often follow in the footsteps of your focus, and what you continuously give your attention to tends to become an ingrained way of being over time. A lot of the time we're not fully aware of what we focus on as we go about daily life and in hard times, often what's pulling at our focus are those ramped-up fear-based patterns of thinking. This means that our thinking is often not unfolding in a helpful way but, once we've become defused, we have the power of choice and can reframe, shifting our focus in the direction we want to go in. The direction of deep resilience.

Let's look now at *how* we can change our focus.

Asking empowering questions

The best way to change our mental focus is through asking ourselves empowering questions. After you have named it and tamed it, you can reframe it by mentally asking yourself (and then answering) questions like:

- What is one small thing I can do to create positive change?

- What's another way of thinking about this that is more useful?

- What is a deeper truth about this situation? My deepest truth?

- What do I really want to feel, create or have here? (Focus less on what you fear or don't like, and more on things that you *do* want to move towards. Eg you could defuse the thought *I hate Mondays* to a new focus of *I wonder how I can make this a really fun, fulfilling and productive week.*)

- Who do I want to be in this moment? (Kind, brave, honest, loving? For instance, when in a difficult chat with a coworker, *I want to be fair, respectful, understanding and find a win-win solution.*)

- How can I make the best of this situation? (A rainy day? Enjoy warm tea, cosy clothes.)

- Who would I be without this thought? (Without the thought, *It's a dreadful day*, explore what's left in your primary experience. It may be simply raining.)

- How can I see this in a different and new way? (If your mind is making up stories, why not make up a new one? *I love the rain; all this abundance watering our gardens, growing our food and filling our tanks. I am blessed.*)

- How can I learn and grow from this?

- What are the different possible ways forward?

- What strengths and resources do I have to help me through?

- What do I need to stay strong, vital and loving?

- How can I use this experience to get stronger, wiser and more loving?

- What new, more enjoyable or empowering story can I create about this situation? (*Mondays are my favourite day of the week – the beginning of a new adventure!*)

- What life-affirming thoughts and actions can I create now?

- What is within my control? What can I *do* to create change for the better?

- How can I have fun doing the things I need to do today?

- What do I appreciate about myself / the other person in this situation?

- How can I care for myself / others in this situation?

- What is my highest intention in this moment?

- What would it look like for me to show up at my best in this situation?

Questions that challenge thoughts

Another way we can use questions to change our focus is to challenge unhelpful thoughts. American author and speaker Byron Katie says a thought is harmless unless we believe it. She argues that it's not our thoughts, but our attachment to our thoughts, that causes suffering.[25] Attaching to a thought is another way to describe fusion – it means believing that it's true, without inquiring into it or gently challenging it. We can challenge a thought by asking ourselves: *Is it true?* and *Is it helpful?* These two questions can help us defuse (or deepen our defusion) from the thought and open up greater mental flexibility and choice.

Remember, when we say 'challenge', we're not talking about going to war with the thought, trying to destroy it or get rid of it. Rather, we are looking to enter a more skilful relationship with our thoughts, allowing us to open ourselves up to freedom and peace of mind, reduce stress and meet our minds with understanding, compassion and wisdom.

Is it true?

One of the simplest ways to let go of (defuse from) an unhelpful thought is to take a closer look at it and gently questioning what evidence there is to support it.

If you ask someone why they believe that something is true, they will give you their collected evidence. You can think of a belief as being like a table, where the legs are the supporting evidence. What makes the table sturdy is the evidence that holds it steady.

My first client, many years ago, was held back by a key belief about herself: 'I'm not smart enough to run my own business.' The table legs of evidence appeared to her to support this: 'I did not do well in certain subjects in school; I don't have any experience; I don't know how to do a business plan; my teacher told me I wouldn't get far in life and she's probably right.'

I asked her to think about what would happen to a table if one of the legs was cut off. It would make the table wobbly, but it might still stand. If you take two legs off, however, it's unlikely to stand. If you continue taking legs off, inevitably the table will fall to the ground. The same happens with our unhelpful stories: once we question the evidence for the thought, we can start to weaken it. It then becomes shaky and, ultimately, collapses.

When asking if something is true, it's helpful to consider:

Is this really true? Can I be 100% sure that this is a cold, hard indisputable truth?

Consider that first client I worked with, years ago – who was actually me! I started to question the key unhelpful belief: I *am not smart enough to run my own business.* Was that actually true? Well, I hadn't even tried to run my own business so I had to admit that I couldn't possibly know if this belief was true unless I went ahead and gave it a try.

Would 100% of people see this the same way?

If you were to take a vote from every single person in the entire world, would all 8.1 billion people have exactly the same viewpoint as you, or is it possible that there is another way to see the situation? If so, consider that the belief might not be 100% true.

Would it hold up in a court of law? If this belief was on trial, would the evidence stack up?

If I tried to convince a judge that I was not smart enough to run a business, would they accept my belief as a cold, hard fact supported by indisputable evidence, or could they argue it with sound reasoning and counterevidence?

If the answer to one or more of these questions is 'No', this supports us to stop holding on to the thought so tightly and opens up the space to defuse from it. Now we understand that the thought is not a fact, we can recognise it as simply an unhelpful thought that the mind has generated to get a sense of certainty. Seeing it for what it is, is liberating.

Is it helpful?

Even if a thought does seem to you to be true, the next, more important question is, *Is this thought useful or helpful to me?*

Some things to consider:

Is this belief/thought helping me to be the person I want to be and live the life I want to live? If it isn't, you don't have to take it seriously or obey it.

Does this thought drive me to take helpful action? If it does not, you can drop it. If you believe and buy into the thought, what could be the results? If you don't like the results, you can let that thought go and focus your mental energy in a more helpful direction.

Remember, we don't have to play out or take seriously every thought that enters our minds (even if we take it to be true). If it is holding you back, you can defuse from and reframe it as needed. After all, thoughts are not reality. They are simply strings of words that arise and pass through our heads – attempts of the mind to make sense of things in ways that may or may not be true, and could be incomplete, inaccurate or entirely made up.

If a thought is not helping you be the person you want to be and live the life you want to live, choose to defuse from it and take meaningful action towards what matters to you, despite what the voice in the head says. Van Gogh once said: 'If you hear a voice within you saying, "You are not a painter," then by all means paint, boy, and that voice will be silenced.'[26] How wonderful that he did paint, despite that voice. We are all blessed by the beauty and creativity he brought to the world, so friend, go ahead and paint when the inner voice says you can't. Ask that person you really like out on a date when the voice tells you it's too scary. And go for that meaningful goal, even if the voice says you can't do it. Keep moving towards the things that truly matter to you deep in your heart.

While none of us is immune to negative thoughts, we all have the ability to continue doing what matters to us *despite* them, and that is the key to living a fulfilling and meaningful life. The negative thoughts will still arise but they won't define you, they won't determine your behaviours and they certainly won't defeat you.

By asking ourselves empowering questions (and coming up with the answers) we reframe our line of thinking and tap into our higher potentials for resilience, resourcefulness, creativity and effectiveness and find greater calm, vitality and a source of strength.

You only need to ask yourself one or two questions at a time, not all of them. Of course, you can also make up your own. The ones above are just examples. Have a bit of fun and bring a bit of playfulness, humour and compassion to your enquiries. One of my clients liked to ask herself, 'What would love do?' as her default question, and she found it was enough to get her through almost anything. The main thing is to remember that when you find your mind tipping into fear-based patterns, you always have the power to change your focus.

EXERCISE 6: Two-minute practice: Defuse and change focus

This practice can take as little as thirty seconds, but usually takes a couple minutes on average.

Think of an unhelpful thought you've had recently.

Got it? Now:

1. Name it. Say to yourself, *Thanks, Mind, but that's not very helpful right now.*

2. Tame it. Bring awareness to the feeling of your breath and take three deep, slow breaths (or use another way of grounding attention).

3. Reframe it. Change focus. Ask and answer one or two of the questions above.

How was this practice for you? What did you notice? Take a moment to contemplate or journal.

You can access a guided audio version of this meditation as well as all the other meditations in this book (and a suite of five other free gifts) at www.melliobrien.com/bookgifts

---

Change the meaning

As we move through life, we have all kinds of experiences, and we all face difficulties, challenges and losses as well as good times. While these undoubtedly all play a role in influencing who we are and how we behave, what *happened* to us is actually far less impactful than the way we *perceive* what happened to us. In other words, our experiences shape us far less than the meanings and stories our mind makes up about these experiences – our beliefs, opinions, judgements and viewpoints.

These are all statements that I have heard from clients struggling to find their way through uncertain and challenging times:

- 'I am a failure.'

- 'This is a disaster.'

- 'I'm unlovable.'

- 'I'll never be the same again.'

- 'Bad things always happen to me.'
- 'I'm not smart enough to run a business.'
- 'I am just a loser.'
- 'Nobody cares about me.'
- 'You can't trust anyone.'
- 'Relationships equal pain.'
- 'People are just selfish. They always hurt you in the end.'
- 'The universe hates me.'
- 'I'm broken now.'

What do these statements all have in common?

Each is a 'disempowering meaning' or what is sometimes referred to as a limiting belief. Unhelpful thoughts like these can sabotage not just your present self, but your future self too. They can exhaust your reserves of inner strength in the present and also, with repetition, hardwire in ways of perceiving the world that diminish your future potential, wellbeing and happiness.

Disempowering meanings can rob you of your courage, grit and power. They can ramp up suffering, drain your vitality and passion and steal your hope. They can crush self-esteem, compel people to give up on their dreams and values, cause anxiety and depression and destroy once-loving relationships.

The great news is, once we are defused from any of these kinds of thoughts, we are already free. But it's not always so easy. Some thoughts have a lot of charge or pull and it can feel tricky to let them go entirely, so we always have the option to reframe the *story* the mind is making out of the thought – to deliberately make more empowering meanings to help us more fully let go of those that are holding us back and unlock and maintain a more robust and adaptive mindset, no matter what life throws our way. Empowering meanings also help us tap into greater inner resources and defuse at a much deeper level so that we break old repeating thoughts and wire in new patterns that help us flourish and stay strong.

The human mind: The meaning-making machine

We know that the mind continually makes up stories in order to make sense of our experiences, and the reason it does this has to do with evolution. As we have learned, the human mind is a survival machine. Its primary goal is your safety and security above all else and it's always focused on keeping you alive.

As our early ancestors went about their daily lives, their minds would be continuously filtering sensory information using two basic (subconscious) questions:

1. *What does it mean? (What is it, and what does it mean for me? Is it a threat or an opportunity?)*

2. *What do I do? (Should I run, fight, hide, eat it, mate with it, use it, stay away from it (pain) or move towards it (pleasure)?)*

The mind is constantly looking for *certainty*. It wants to know and understand everything that is happening in your sensory field so that it can protect you and keep you alive. That's why it is asking those two simple questions and that is also why it is constantly commentating on your life – judging, labelling, analysing, assessing and asserting viewpoints and opinions. It's trying to make sense and meaning out of all that sensory data so you can figure out how to navigate it all.

The big challenge is that it doesn't just want certainty, it wants certainty *fast*. This means that those narratives we are making about the world around us are often both snap judgements and generalisations. They are a quick attempt to piece things together so that we can respond quickly. The mind has a rule for this process: speed trumps accuracy.

For our hunter-gatherer ancestors, it was far better to make a fast judgement that enabled them to act quickly, even if that judgement later turned out not to be totally accurate. If there was a rustle in the bushes, better to assume it was a tiger and run rather than waste time worrying about whether your judgement was correct. Second-guessing a snap judgement could get you eaten!

The problem for us now is that these instinctive snap judgements, which are often incomplete and inaccurate, can be limiting, disempowering and cause us to suffer. They can also cause a lot of reactivity, misunderstanding and conflict.

Meaning making in action

Read the following story slowly, line by line:

Johnny was on his way to school.
He was worried about the maths lesson.
He was not sure he could control the class
again today.
It was not part of a janitor's duty.

What did you notice happening in your mind as you read each sentence? Most people find that they repeatedly updated their view of what is happening: first, they assume Johnny is a young student, then a teacher and, finally, he becomes a janitor.

This example illustrates how our mind is continuously working behind the scenes to build a mental picture of our experiences. We rarely, if ever, experience life as it truly is, taking an objective overview of each situation. Instead, we experience it through a series of mental inferences based on the information that is available to us at any moment.

The mind elaborates on that information, generating stories to attach to it, continuously making assumptions based on past experiences and anticipating what it will mean in the future. As a result, events experienced in the mind's eye can end up differing massively from one person to the next and from objective 'reality'. The story above demonstrates a simple point about the way our mind jumps to conclusions: we often get things wrong.

On any given day, the mind is constantly making guesses, assumptions and predictions about the world and other people, and we're barely conscious of it. Some of these make a positive difference in the way we live, and some are neutral in the way they affect us. Many of these assumptions will be unhelpful, however, and can lead to stress, disempowerment, conflict, confusion and suffering.

Have you ever seen a director's commentary on a film where they talk about what was involved in its making while the movie plays muted in the background? This is actually a good analogy for what it's like living with a human mind. We have our direct experience – our primary experience. This is the *actual* experience of our lives – what we see, feel, hear, smell and taste, our sense perceptions. Then we have that mental commentary – secondary experience – playing continuously as well.

In difficult times, the mind tends not only to tip our focus in unhelpful directions but also to tell us disempowering stories. Some are old stories we've been telling ourselves for a long time and we easily fall into the same old patterns, but it can also create new unhelpful meanings. Even though your mind is only trying to make sense out of the world in an attempt to protect you, it may generate thoughts that shut down your heart, close your mind, flare your hostility and distrust and lock you into a dark and disempowering outlook on life.

All of this can make a difficult time much, much harder.

This is a good moment to ponder, what are some of the meanings you have been making about yourself, life or other people that are potentially not so helpful and not so empowering?

EXERCISE 7: Three-minute exercise: The ocean of awareness

Take a moment to focus on the feeling of your breathing. Place your hands on your heart and feel the rising and falling sensation of the breath flowing in... and out. Do this for a few breaths. Try to have the sense of becoming the depths of the ocean of awareness rather than the waves of thought and emotion.

Then ask yourself, what are some beliefs, stories, judgements, assumptions or viewpoints that the mind has generated in the past in an attempt to keep you safe, but which now no longer serve you?

Thank the mind for trying to protect you, let it know it did a great job. But also tell it if this isn't helpful anymore.

Then acknowledge that these are simply thoughts, mental events generated by the mind in an attempt to protect you. They are not reality. They are small passing waves in the vast depths of who you are.

Building a relationship with your mind where you, as the observer of it, are a friend, wise elder, leader, parent and partner, allows the mind to relax its fear circuitry, and find more useful and helpful ways to navigate through life.

You can access a guided audio version of this meditation as well as all the other meditations in this book at www. melliobrien.com/bookgifts

---

Make more empowering meaning

When we realise that we can make our own meanings, we can choose ways of thinking that are supportive and empowering. Disempowering meanings like, 'I am a loser,' 'I am not attractive enough,' 'I cannot make relationships work,' 'People are all selfish deep down,' can feel true when we repeat them over and over to ourselves and hold onto them tightly. They feel familiar and generate familiar feelings. But the cost of holding onto them is high. Increased suffering. Diminished performance and potential. Meaningful goals never achieved. Stagnated healing. Getting stuck in painful or harmful patterns. Loss of relationships, happiness and even health.

But if we are willing to let go of what is no longer serving us, we can open up to profound inner transformation, deep healing, new vistas of possibility and potential as well as greater freedom and peace of mind.

Here are some common situations and experiences with examples of how they can be reframed; first is a disempowering meaning, and then a reframed meaning.

After a big setback:

I'm ruined.   vs   That was a setback, but I
                                     learned a lot and I know what
                                     to do differently next time.

After being badly treated:

You can't trust anyone.   vs   I'm disappointed and hurt by this person's actions. I'll set stronger boundaries and have a clear and honest talk with them about how I feel.

After making a mistake:

I'm such an idiot. I always mess things up. I'll never get this right.   vs   I'm human. We all make mistakes sometimes. I've also had many successes. Every mistake is a learning opportunity.

After going through a painful loss:

I can't cope with this.   vs   I've got this. I have all the resources I need to navigate this. I'll just take it one step and one day at a time.

Trying to achieve a meaningful goal:

I'll never be able to do that.   vs   I'm committed to doing whatever it takes.

After a breakup:

I just can't 'do' relationships.   vs   I've learned a lot about how to have happier and healthier relationships and I'll take this wisdom forward into my next relationship.

View of life:

Life's a bitch and then you die.	vs	Life is a grand adventure and deep mystery. It's a privilege to be here.

After a failed attempt at winning in competition:

I'm a loser. It's hopeless. This is never going to work.	vs	I never lose. I either win or I learn. I get stronger with every attempt.

The 'changing the meaning' part of the 'reframe it' step involves making new helpful meanings that unlock our greater qualities and potential, lift our mood, bolster our resilience and help us take empowered action. We can consciously choose to replace limiting beliefs with empowering ones – and why not? The mind is making up stories all the time, so why not consciously create some that feel truer, more uplifting and supportive – beliefs that make us mentally stronger, happier, more connected and more able to live our life on purpose?

When my mind told my younger self, *You're not smart enough to run a business*, I countered it with a more empowering belief: *I'll never know if I'm smart enough until I try.* That felt more honest and helpful. I then tried out an additional belief: *Anyone is smart enough to run a company with enough determination, passion and focus.* That felt truer than the limiting belief I started with, and I also found more evidence to support it. I held it close and here I am, years later, running my business and sharing these tools with you.

One of my clients, Amanda, had a limiting story she had been telling herself for years: *I'm broken*. When she questioned it, she realised that not only was she still standing after her traumatic experience, she was actually helping others because of it. She had turned her pain into purpose. She realised, *I'm not broken, I'm stronger than I've ever been before. I'm a powerful healer.* Then she even felt a sense of gratitude for what she had been through. It had motivated her to help people. The new meaning she had made felt truer to her than her initial belief and she found more evidence to support it.

Another client of mine, Sam, believed that the universe hated her. She felt she had evidence to support this: the universe hadn't given her the relationship she wanted, her business had failed, she didn't have the kind of money she wanted, and so on. As a result, she felt bitter and jaded. When she questioned that belief, however, she had to acknowledge that the universe couldn't hate at all – it didn't have a mind to hate with, as far as she knew. From there, she began to focus on all that the universe *had* given her – lungs to breathe with, eyes to see with, ears to hear her favourite music and the morning birdsong with, food to enjoy and many people who cared about her. It had given her the most precious thing of all: life. She arrived at the conclusion that the universe is abundant and supportive if you just pay attention, and this led to a profound mindset shift, leading to much more joy, appreciation and contentment in her life from then on.

I invite you to go for it – try now to create a more empowering meaning for yourself. Aim to find your way to a new meaning that is helpful and also feels genuinely true for you. Here I've provided some prompts to help you.

What's your deepest truth about this situation?

Say you had a difficult interaction with someone and your mind made the meaning, *They're just a jerk*. Imagine now that you explored what the deeper truth of the situation might be. Maybe you consider a deeper truth such as, 'Everyone is just doing their best with the resources that they have.' In other words, this person, with all their previous conditioning, level of awareness and the current circumstances of their life, is simply trying to get by and you don't know the whole story of what is going on for them.

You might also consider whether this person is truly 'just a jerk' twenty-four hours a day, every day. Have they never done anything kind for anyone? Is that really the whole story? Maybe upon deeper consideration you come to the belief that, deep down, everyone is trying their best to be happy, safe and get through life. Ultimately, there's no such thing as a jerk, just people who are not able to be at their best, who are confused, stuck in old patterns or hurting, maybe just having a bad day, and they all deserve our compassion and kindness.

What's a meaning that sounds opposite to the original meaning but actually rings true, or truer?

Consider these examples of opposing beliefs:

Not smart enough   vs   Anyone can run a business with enough determination

Damaged   vs   Not damaged, stronger than ever

The universe hates me   vs   The universe is supportive and abundant

Experiment with taking on a totally opposing thought to your original limiting belief and then try to find as much evidence to support it as possible. We're not trying to fool ourselves – we're just unwinding the BS (belief system) that the mind unconsciously created in the first place. We're updating our programming so we can adapt and thrive in the times and environment that we're living in now. We're consciously creating an alternative and more empowering lens through which we choose to see and interact with the world.

What's a more empowering belief you'd like to enjoy instead?

Maybe instead of waking up and instantly thinking, *Mondays suck!*, you'd like to think, *Ah, Mondays! The start of an adventure. I wonder where we'll go this week*? You may as well have some fun with it and make stories that nourish you, lift you up and empower you.

Remember playful curiosity. Don't be afraid to be creative. Do this with humour, warmth and a sense of exploration.

Becoming more yourself

We can become extremely invested in maintaining our mind's storylines and conditioning. They can feel like a part of our identity because we have held onto them for so long. They are familiar and safe, and can feel like our emotional and mental home. Because of this, it's not always easy to let them go, but our ability to become deeply resilient, rise to our challenges and live the life that's true to us depends on our courage and willingness to put down those old storylines and start choosing more empowering, authentic ways of being.

To be deeply resilient, we need to get comfortable with being more flexible, fluid and discerning with our thinking patterns. When unhelpful conditioning is playing out, defuse and shift your thoughts, trusting your deeper nature as the authority and the ultimate guide for how to live your life. The result is that you will *become more authentic, more yourself.*

By letting go of disempowering, limiting or unhelpful stories, challenges can turn into opportunities, mistakes into learning moments and a painful past into a positive future. Anxiety can shift into courage or excitement, lack into gratitude, fear into power and loneliness into love. Such is the power of making empowering meanings.

The meanings you make and the words you use can be the difference between strength and suffering. They can form a cage that holds you back and shuts you down or the catalyst for unlocking your authenticity and potential, opening and freeing your heart and mind.

In this step you have learned how to defuse and reframe thoughts that are taking you away from inner strength, by changing your focus and changing the meaning you give them, shifting unhelpful thoughts and replacing them with others that are more supportive. Taking control in this way will lead you to becoming more of the person you truly want to be and enjoying the life you actually want to live.

Summary

Through the lessons and exercises of this chapter, building on those in previous chapters, you have now built a strong foundation to go on to master Step 1 of the Deep Resilience Method: Recognise and Regulate your Thoughts and Emotions. You now know how to be self-compassionate, how to approach your mind and the world in a whole new way – with greater understanding, skill, kindness and acceptance, allowing you to regulate it in ways that release you from suffering, help you reclaim your power and take effective action.

A powerful transformation is already taking place, where those fear-based thoughts won't be able to take over in the same way as before and these foundational tools set you up to find more stability, confidence and clarity, and you can now lean on them for support when you need to.

6
Wage Peace

Sue held her head in her hands as she spoke to me, her body was tense, her breathing shallow. Her slow, stuttering words filled with anguish. 'This shouldn't be happening. I haven't done anything to deserve this.' A brief pause. Then she quietly moaned, 'Why me? I just want this to go away,' and started to cry. Sue had recently been diagnosed with a degenerative illness and was understandably feeling anger, fear, shock and sadness. Of course, Sue wanted so badly for things to be different to how they were. None of us would ever wish for a diagnosis like that. But unfortunately, we cannot control everything that happens to us, and when we mentally resist what is happening, we create much more suffering for ourselves. Sue had been caught in a tailspin of racing thoughts and resistance and inner struggle for days and was feeling more and more exhausted, overwhelmed and frantic.

Resistance is a basic pattern of thinking that involves struggling against or refusing to accept the way things are and wanting things to be different. While it's totally understandable that we would want to get away from painful or unpleasant things, resistance doesn't actually help us because it only throws fuel on the fire of our suffering.

Psychological suffering comes in many forms, as we have seen. The mind can play out all kinds of patterns that deepen instead of relieving our distress, but when we are going through tough times, the bulk of our suffering is usually caused by mental resistance. In fact, in a talk by renowned spiritual teacher Eckhart Tolle he estimated that around 95% of all suffering likely comes from mental resistance.[27] That may sound like an incredible claim but in my experience over the years, working with so many people (and my own mind), this resonates with me as a pretty fair estimate. The good news is that if an enormous amount of our suffering originates from this way of being with our difficult experiences, by understanding and identifying mental resistance and learning how to work with it in a new and more helpful way, we can have a huge impact on our state of mind and our quality of life, especially in difficult times.

Resistance might sound something like:

- *This isn't fair.*
- *Why me?*

- *I can't cope with this.*

- *I hate this.*

- *I want this to end.*

- *This shouldn't be happening.*

- *That shouldn't have happened in the past.*

- *Screw this/them (or another swear word or phrase).*

- *I don't want this.*

- *Why did they do this to me?*

- *This sucks.*

These are just some basic examples, but mental resistance can take many different forms. All of them involve wishing or wanting the present moment to be different than it is. This basic non-acceptance of what already is, is futile. Not only that, but the more strongly you resist what is happening in the present moment, the more suffering and stress you experience and the more fused and reactive you tend to become.

Acceptance is power

Acceptance is the antidote to resistance. It does not mean resignation, passivity or giving up. Acceptance is simply the attitude of allowing things to be as they are instead of resisting them. It's the choice to let go of psychological suffering and wage peace, instead of war, with the way things are. It means acknowledging what is true in the moment. That doesn't mean you have to pretend you like it or want it, but rather that you simply make peace with the way things are.

There are two main reasons that acceptance is so powerful as a way of relating to our circumstances. The first is that it alleviates a huge amount of our inner turmoil and anguish. The second is because it gives us more choice. Not more choice in what happens to us but in how we respond to what happens. Returning to the mental strength line we learned about earlier, acceptance is another practice we can use to defuse and shift back above the line. Once we're above it, we have more choice and while we can't escape all pain, we can let go of any unnecessary suffering caused by resistance and thought fusion, and then we can free up our inner resources so that we act intentionally, wisely and effectively to meet our challenges.

For instance, you might feel annoyed when you're caught in a traffic jam or when the weather is cold and rainy, but through acceptance we can start to see that getting annoyed by such things isn't helpful. No matter how frustrated and impatient we become, we will not change the weather or move the traffic forward. We just end up below the line, adding more suffering to an unpleasant but unavoidable situation. Not only that, but our bad mood may start to then leak into other areas of our life, diminishing our focus, performance and effectiveness at work, creating conflict in relationships and affecting our mental and emotional wellbeing.

In resistance, we're below the line, fused with thoughts and so we become more reactive. We often feel like it's the only possible reaction to have in the given situation. We tend to play out the same patterns we always do. We just assume traffic jams equal irritation. Bad weather equals bad mood. A big setback equals anxiety. A blunt comment from our partner equals anger and resentment. We feel we have no choice in the matter.

However, if we were to look around on that rainy day, we might see that some people are happily splashing in the puddles on the way to work, and some might be going about their day totally unconcerned by it, laughing at jokes, enjoying hot drinks and watching the rain. We start to see that there are many different ways to respond to a given situation. We don't have to react in the way we always do and we don't have to play out our negative thoughts.

Once we understand that our annoyance, our grumpiness or our anxiety is not *caused* by the rain, the traffic or the setback itself but by our reaction to it, then the ability to *choose* a new response arises. We become more psychologically flexible.

We can ask ourselves, *Will I buy into and play out these thoughts and go along the path that I know leads to annoyance or unhelpful actions, or shall I choose to respond in a different way, one that alleviates suffering and helps me thrive?*

Acceptance is power. From the state of acceptance, you can let go of suffering and reactivity and find new flexible, creative, empowered and compassionate ways forward.

Reacting vs responding

Let's return for a moment to the difference between reacting and responding, which we touched on earlier in the book. In the sport of bull fighting, a matador understands the difference between reacting and responding all too well because for them, it could be a matter of life or death. For a matador, the key to winning the fight against an animal that is much stronger, larger and more powerful than them is simple. They must keep the bull distracted, stressed and reactive by hustling it around the arena constantly. They must do all they can to stop the bull from having a moment to pause and find focus.

But if the bull does find just a moment to physically stop and regain his composure, he gathers his wits, remember his own strength and takes back his power. It is at this point that the matador will become extremely nervous, for they will have lost control and the bull has become much more dangerous.

In the same way the bull can find his point of power in the middle of a highly stressful situation, so can we. We find our power (to respond and not react) by entering the state of acceptance of what is.

When we are below the line and fused with our thoughts, we are reactive. A reaction is generally not conscious. Rather, it's automatic and habitual. A response, however, is conscious, intentional and creative. When stuck in a traffic jam, for instance, instead of sitting there cursing the other drivers, berating yourself and feeling wrapped up in annoyance and irritation (reaction), you intentionally accept the situation, defuse from the thoughts creating stress and then you're free to choose a response. Perhaps you consider how you might enjoy that moment by putting a podcast on, calling an old friend or appreciating the view out the window. Whatever you do, you do it from a place of inner acceptance, working with the flow of life not against it.

The first step in moving from reaction to response is to recognise resistance when it arises, which it very likely will when you're going through a hard time. If you're anything like me or anyone else with a normal human mind, you will probably find it difficult initially, to accept the situation, especially if the traffic is blocking you from getting to an important meeting or the rain is on your wedding day. Let alone getting a diagnosis that changes your entire life.

Unpleasant emotions and thoughts naturally arise in response to unwanted or painful experiences, and it is often a very quick and automatic response. We may not have any more control over how we initially feel than we do over the events that are unfolding, but we can also accept our initial emotional responses with as much compassion, grace and friendliness as possible.

Judging or berating ourselves for having normal human emotional reactions is not helpful. Accepting them as a part of the present moment can shift us back above the line, into greater awareness, more flexibility and inner peace.

The mantra of inner peace

If we can notice when resistance is arising, we can defuse from it. We have our defusion tools for this, but we also need to add in a deliberate attitude of acceptance.

When we are resisting or struggling against our experience, we become exhausted, reactive and we suffer. Knowing this, let's look at how applying acceptance to the situation is a much more adaptive response.

Sometimes acceptance can be tricky, especially in the face of big challenges, so it helps to have a mantra to lean on, to help you let go of resistance. The one I like to use, myself and with clients, I call the 'mantra of inner peace'. Say to yourself: *Right now, it's like this.* Or you can try, *It's OK for this to be here.*

Acceptance allows you to stop going to war with what is and make peace with it instead. With it, you can drop the struggle, alleviate stress and suffering and open up your point of power (the power to respond).

Once you accept (by saying the manta of inner peace), bring your focus back to your primary experience – become present in the moment and connected to your senses. At first it can be a little bit tricky to let go of resistance (secondary experience) and ground yourself back in the present moment and in your senses (primary experience). It is especially hard when we're in a situation that is highly stressful or that triggers us and where we tend to react, so be patient with and kind to yourself and keep practising acceptance as much as you can. Each time you do this, you create new neural pathways in your brain that increase your inner peace and strength and decrease negativity and stress. Every single practice makes you stronger.

EXERCISE 8: Three-minute exercise: Practise letting go of resistance

Settle into a comfortable position and, when you're ready, start to scan through your present moment experience for anything that's a little bit unpleasant. It doesn't have to be something big; it could be something as small as an itch, a feeling of tiredness, or a sound that you would prefer not to be there.

See if you can turn your attention gently towards it and just have an attitude of allowing it to be there. Make peace with it. Let go of any sense of agitation with it, any tension. Try the mantra of inner peace – *Right now, it's like this*, or, *It's OK for this to be here.*

Now shift your focus to primary experiences (if you're not sure where to focus, feel your breath). See if you can get a sense of relaxing into the moment, allowing the pleasant and unpleasant to be there and meeting it all with an accepting and kindly awareness.

What did you notice? Many clients notice that the mind settles and becomes calmer when they practise acceptance, and some notice a release of physical tension in the body. Others report a significant sense of relief. You may have noticed greater mental clarity as you opened up the mental space to have more awareness.

Don't worry if you didn't experience these things, as it's different for everybody, but do rest assured that with practice, acceptance becomes easier and easier and mental clarity, steadiness and confidence when faced with difficulty will become more and more accessible.

You can access a guided audio version of this meditation (as well as all the other meditations in this book and some additional resources) at www.melliobrien.com/bookgifts

---

Accept, then act

Once we have stopped resisting, accepted our situation and connected with awareness, we are now above the line and are able to *respond* more wisely and effectively if action is needed.

An important and useful thing to do to regain resilience and power is to focus on what is within your control, and then take action. Remember, you cannot always control what happens but in any given situation, you can control your attitude, your words and your actions.

It's like the serenity prayer – accept the things you cannot change and change the things you can.[28] In tough times, make peace with what you cannot control, think about who you would like to be in this situation, what would be helpful, and what matters to you most – and then act. More on this later in the book.

Summary

Letting go of resistance and shifting into acceptance allows us to respond (not react) from a state of greater awareness. In this shift we find our point of power. We ease suffering, regain mental clarity and are able to choose helpful actions instead of playing out old reactions and patterns. Whenever you find yourself feeling anger, grief, fear, overwhelm, resentment, distress or reactivity, I encourage you, friend, to remember, and return to, over and over, your point of power – the point from which you can respond and make conscious choices. The place where you can find greater peace and freedom.

Whenever resistance arises, repeat the mantra of inner peace, make peace with yourself and life as it is and then, if needed, act with awareness.

7
Overcoming Overthinking

U ncertainty, change and challenges have always
been part of human life – a new romance, a new
job, your first baby, the death of someone close, the
loss of a business, a serious diagnosis, a divorce, and
so on. In 2020, however, the entire world was plunged
into an unprecedented level of deep uncertainty that
shook us all and brought the world as we knew it to a
grinding halt.

During the years when the pandemic was at its
height, we didn't know when (or even if) we would
be able to leave our homes again, return to work,
take a vacation, go to a restaurant or even see our
loved ones. Businesses went bust, funerals, births and
weddings were missed, and tragically, a significant
number of lives were lost. We didn't know if we were
safe from the pandemic and none of us knew when

things would return to normal, or if, indeed, they ever would.

Uncertainty can sometimes be pleasant and positive, but when it's unexpected and unwanted, it can throw us into a mental tailspin of suffering, anxiety and disempowerment right when what we need most is empowerment, calm, clarity and resilience in the face of unforeseen situations or circumstances.

When we go through any kind of crisis or challenge, it's important to know that a certain amount of stress and anxiety are normal and natural responses to any kind of event that threatens our safety or is difficult, painful or precarious. It's also normal to want to spend some time figuring out our problems, thinking through our next steps or trying to learn from our mistakes. However, it is in the face of adversity and uncertainty that our minds tip into a state of fixation (on our problems) and hypervigilance. We become stuck in overthinking – lost in swarms of racing, looping and spinning thoughts that can feel like a mental fog or a constant background radiation of stress. Worry and rumination, the most common forms of overthinking, can feel like they are hijacking our minds (as in fact they are, as we shall see) and can increase our risk of tipping into chronic mental health issues like depression, chronic stress and ongoing anxiety.

In this chapter, we will learn how to break the overthinking habit and focus the mind's abilities on more helpful, flexible and skilful strategies for dealing with life's uncertainties.

Understanding overthinking

The mind engages in overthinking because it thinks it will serve a helpful purpose: to try to regain a sense of control, to keep us safe, to learn from our mistakes, to solve problems and figure out next steps. So we may find ourselves ruminating about the past, stewing on our problems all day and playing out all the stories and 'what if' scenarios about the future again and again.

In any kind of uncertain, threatening or challenging situation, overthinking tends to kick in because of that survival-based conditioning of the mind. The inner guard dog, roused from its sleep, senses a threat and goes into high alert to try to protect us and regain some control. The problem is that the vast majority of the time, these instinctive survival responses have exactly the opposite effect of their intended purpose. Instead of helping us to feel calmer and more in control, to think more clearly and take more effective action, the more we overthink things, the more stressed, frantic, overwhelmed, powerless and out of control we're likely to feel, as we have seen. Overthinking is a habit that saps our resilience, keeps us stuck in a state of fusion and pulls us below the line. It is also strongly linked to depression, anxiety and burnout.[29]

To make things worse, overthinking grows like a rolling snowball. The more you do it, the more fused you become and the more the unhelpful thoughts come. Before you know it, your mind is racing and the big mass of tension, fear, overwhelm and anxiety expands ever outward. These are the extra layers of suffering we tend to pile on top of our already existing difficulties. They ramp up the fear circuitry of the mind, wear us down and disable our ability to take empowered action. We do, however, have a choice in how we respond to uncertainty: we can ride the wave of change instead of letting it crash down upon us.

The weight of the glass

Overthinking might seem harmless enough. What's the problem in having a little extra thought? But carrying the mental weight of ongoing fusion with thoughts is no small matter. This story illustrates why.

A psychology professor was teaching a class one day. At one point, she raised a glass of water and asked the audience, 'How heavy is this glass of water?'

The students started shouting out their guesses.

After a while she said to them, 'You know, the total weight of this glass doesn't really matter. What matters is how long I keep holding it.

'If I hold this glass for a minute or so, it's pretty light and holding it is pretty easy but if I hold it for an hour with my arm out like this, that's really going to start to burn. If I hold this glass for a day, it's going to be agonising. At some point, my arm would probably become paralysed. It wouldn't be able to function anymore and the glass would smash on the floor, as I would be unable to hold it any longer.

'The weight of the glass in each of these lengths of time didn't change, but the longer I held it, the heavier and harder it felt,' she said.

This glass of water is like your stressful thoughts. Think about them for a while and that's going to feel OK. Think about them a little bit more – that's going to begin to burn a little. Think about them all day long, every day, and you will probably feel consumed by suffering and stress. You probably won't enjoy life much anymore. You could even end up at the point where you crash completely or become so paralysed by the suffering and stress that you're incapable of getting on with your life as you'd wish to until you learn to stop carrying the weight of all those thoughts.

We all overthink things from time to time. It's hard not to, but when we start to get stuck in this pattern it can come at a great cost. Unfortunately, these repetitive thinking patterns are particularly easy to slip into when stressed or going through a big challenge. Whether you are beating yourself up for a mistake you made last week, obsessing over something for tomorrow, or worrying about what people think of you or what might happen, overthinking everything can be debilitating.

Researchers have found that overthinking can have real impacts on our wellbeing and ability to cope and stay resilient in challenging times. It does so in a number of different ways:

- It increases emotional distress and your chance of developing mental illness. Studies have demonstrated a strong link between overthinking and the development of depression and anxiety.[30]

- It can set up a vicious cycle: when you overthink, your mental health starts to decline; as your mental health declines, your tendency to overthink increases. To escape the distress caused by that cycle, many overthinkers default to unhelpful coping strategies such as abusing alcohol or drugs or overeating.[31]

- Worry impairs critical thinking and problem-solving ability. Overthinkers often feel like they're helping themselves by ruminating or worrying so much but research shows that overthinking makes you more reactive and gets in the way of effective problem solving and skilful action.[32]

- It impairs your sleep. Studies confirm (as does our first-hand experience – we've all had one of those nights!) that overthinking significantly disrupts sleep.[33] When racing thoughts elicit a fight-or-flight response, you'll often find yourself tossing and turning for hours. When you do eventually get to sleep, it may not be that refreshing because overthinking also impairs the quality and depth of your sleep. Before long, these effects can make you feel drained, foggy-headed and fatigued.

Regulating overthinking

The part of your brain that controls your ability to reason and think clearly and objectively can get hijacked when strong emotions like fear, anxiety or anger trigger the brain's fight-or-flight response. Early humans were constantly exposed to potential threats of harm or death. To improve chances of survival, the fight-or-flight response evolved. It's an automatic response to physical danger that allows you to react quickly without thinking by sending out signals to release stress hormones that prepare your body to fight or run as fast as you can.

The fight-or-flight response can also be triggered by psychological threats, such as an unhelpful, negative or stress-filled thoughts. Or it could be a small thing, like a blunt text message, a funny look from someone or a late train, that triggers the mind to start overthinking and flooding it with alarm.

A part of your brain called the amygdala then kicks into action. The amygdala can disable the brain's frontal lobes, the more evolved areas of the brain responsible for higher-level thinking and reasoning, what some refer to as the 'smart part' of our brain. When this happens, it's incredibly difficult to think clearly, make rational decisions or control your responses. Control has been 'hijacked' by the amygdala. Now instead of responding effectively to your situation, you're more likely to react. You're more likely to feel out of control, have intense emotional outbursts, lash out, do and say things you'll regret later and get thrown around by powerful emotions and impulses.

Overthinking starts with an innocent desire to solve problems and make informed predictions so that we can increase our chance of survival, security and safety, but continuing the cycle of overthinking perpetuates the fight-or-flight response and can keep us stuck in a loop of reactivity, anxiety, exhaustion and negativity.

Seeing this clearly, we can understand that for most of the problems we face these days we need a different type of mindset, a different approach and different solutions. If we want to be able to respond effectively, stay calm under pressure and protect our wellbeing, it's vital that we can recognise and regulate overthinking.

EXERCISE 9: Two-minute breathwork practice: Down-regulate the nervous system

Any time you feel caught up and reactive, you can shift out the body's fight-or-flight response and down-regulate your nervous system (calming the amygdala and bringing your critical thinking capacity back online). You can do this in two simple steps.

First, mentally naming the emotion you're feeling and then second, taking some slow deep belly breaths. Ideally five to ten breaths.

I invite you to try this now. To begin with, take a moment to remember a time when you felt stress, anger or reactivity and perhaps started overthinking. Think the way you thought then and bring those emotions to mind.

Got it? Now mentally name the emotion you're currently feeling; for example, *Stress is here*, or, *I feel angry*. Aim to bring the attitude of acceptance to the emotion as you say it.

Next, take five to ten slow deep belly breaths. The breath should feel comfortable and not strained. You can place a hand on the belly if you find that helpful. As you breathe out, see if you can let go of some tension or tightness in the body. Relax as much as you can through your jaw, shoulders, hands, belly and whole body.

What did you notice? Many people notice a feeling of greater calm and steadiness in their body and mind. Others find that they are able to think more clearly and feel centred again. This is because through mental naming and deep breathing you can down-regulate, or even turn off, the body's fight-or-flight response and simultaneously bring your brain's higher capacities (frontal cortex) back online. This practice can be done in as little as 30 seconds and is a useful technique to enable you to find your centre and strength in any kind of stressful situation.

You can access a guided audio version of this meditation (as well as all the other meditations and some additional resources) at www.melliobrien.com/bookgifts

Identifying overthinking

When it comes to being able to defuse from unhelpful thinking patterns, the key first step is being able to recognise when it is happening. The two main types of overthinking are rumination and worry, so let's take a closer look at each of them.

Worry

Worry is when you cast your mind into the future and imagine what could go wrong. It may involve playing out 'what if' scenarios about the future or catastrophising about the present, which is often perceived as considerably worse than it actually is.

'Worry,' says author and spiritual teacher Eckhart Tolle, 'pretends to be necessary but serves no useful purpose.'[34] Tolle is noting that, although the human mind is great at thinking through different ways of solving a problem, running different scenarios of what could happen in the future and planning accordingly, it often continues this pattern beyond what is useful and then, as we've seen, it becomes unhelpful, painful and even debilitating.

Worry is when you are dwelling on a problem or a situation, thinking about it over and over again but without any real intention to solve it, learn from it or figure out best next steps in that moment. Instead, you are just chewing on it like a dog with a bone, rolling it around in your mind and stewing on it. You are fused with it.

Worry might sound something like this:

- *What if it floods again? I don't think I can handle it again. It would be a disaster.*

- *What if my business never gets off the ground? I'll be a failure. I'll be ruined.*

- *My boss looked at me weirdly the other day, maybe he's going to fire me.*

- *If I can't get some sleep then tomorrow will be a write-off and I'll never finish that project.*

- *After the argument today that new colleague probably hates me and will tell everyone what an idiot I am and ruin my reputation.*

- *I have a weird spot on my leg. It's probably cancer. I could die. What will happen to my kids?*

- *They're all going to laugh at me. I'll make a fool of myself if I try this. It's never going to work.*

- *Why is my partner not home yet? They must be having an affair, or perhaps they've been caught up in a terrible accident and are lying in a ditch somewhere and will never be found?*

Worry can also take the form of imagining visual scenes of things going wrong, however unlikely or implausible they might be. My mind often does this when my cat has been outside for a couple of hours. I find myself imagining scenes where he has been bitten by a snake, hit by a car or attacked by another cat. When this happens, I start to feel increasingly anxious, only for him to wander in ten minutes later and happily rub himself on my leg, as unbothered as only cats can be!

Rumination

The other most common type of overthinking – rumination – is engaging in a repetitive negative thought process about a problem, flaw, mistake, embarrassment, misfortune or regret. It is usually about an event from the past and tends to loop continuously through your mind.

Rumination often involves a looping replay of scenes from unpleasant events or missed opportunities. It might sound something like this:

- *I'm so stupid for making that comment at the work Xmas party. It's going to be awful when I go back to work. I am probably going to get fired now.*

- *Why do these things always have to happen to me?*

- *I made a big mistake five years ago when I left my wife. My life is ruined now. I'll never recover.*

- *I'm just a loser. I've never amounted to anything.*

- *Why do I always make the same mistakes? What's wrong with me? How could I be so stupid?*

- *How could they do this to me? I've been nothing but nice to them. I don't deserve this.*

- *This thing happened to me and now I can never be happy.*

Rumination can contribute to the development of anxiety or depression,[35] and is characterised by the mind dwelling on a problem, situation or concern without a true intention to solve it, learn from it, heal, make peace with it or figure out helpful next steps. We are fused with the thoughts and dwelling on the problem but not in a useful or constructive way, and it's ramping up stress and suffering, pulling us below the mental strength line.

Moving beyond overthinking

You already have the tools to help you work with unhelpful thinking patterns in general, with the Name It, Tame It, Reframe It practice. Now you can add two more targeted tools to your toolbox – these are specialised techniques to shift anxiety and rumination into empowerment, effectiveness and wisdom.

Constructive problem solving

Professors at university hold office hours once or twice a week. They don't give their students twenty-four-seven access to them. This is because it would become totally overwhelming and debilitating if students could access them at any time they wished, day or night, and the professors would never be able to get any other work done. The same is true of our mind: if we give our worries, rumination and self-doubt twenty-four-seven access to our attention, it will be just as debilitating and destructive. We won't be able to focus properly and we'll quickly become overwhelmed and stressed.

What if, like those professors, we set aside scheduled office hours for our thinking through our problems and plans? We could make a deal with ourselves to allocate a small amount of time every day/week to do some focused and constructive thinking about what could happen in the future or how we want to handle our current problems. After office hours, we defuse and let it go.

If we find ourselves ruminating or worrying outside our agreed office hours, we can give ourselves permission to leave it for now, knowing that there is a designated time and space to deal with it later. You can use the great defusing tools you already have available to you to let go of those thoughts for now.

Keeping to office hours will help free you from the habit of overthinking. It will give you the space to deal with life's challenges in a more clear-headed, calm and effective way and you will feel more in control in everyday life.

Take the Lesson, Move On

In hard times, we can often get caught up in ruminating on regrets, misfortunes and mistakes we've made in the past. Wishing things could have been different.

This kind of rumination is a funny thing because even though we know that no matter how much we sit there and wish things went differently in the past, it doesn't change anything. It's a strange habit because regret and rumination don't feel good – they cause us to suffer – and yet we can't seem to help replaying these thoughts again and again, beating ourselves up about the way things went or hating that it happened that way.

We get caught back in time, remembering our mistakes or painful moments, whether it was blurting out something insensitive, an embarrassing incident, a heartbreaking moment or one of reactivity or anger. We often beat ourselves up for our mistakes or rage against reality, then feel shame, negativity or hopelessness.

Doing this is not useful or helpful for us. We don't learn much from it and we don't grow, we just generate a lot of extra inner turmoil, so why is the human mind so prone to this habit? Again, it's because of how we evolved. For our hunter-gatherer ancestors, life was difficult and dangerous and so to survive, it was important for them to remember and learn as much as possible from any dangerous encounters such as a run-in with a bear or a rival clan. By replaying the event again and again, they could learn from it and have a better chance of surviving a similar encounter next time.

The modern mind still tends to do the same thing, but now the situations usually have far lower stakes and so the mind tends to take this tendency way beyond what is actually useful. Getting stuck in these unhelpful thought loops is painful. It can drag down our self-esteem, disempower us, keep us up at night, crush our confidence and even pull us into depression.

There is a way to work with regret in a healthy and helpful way, though, and that is by using a practice I call Take the Lesson, Move On. This two-step technique will give you a targeted way to relieve rumination and help you take a step back from the painful memory so you can choose to approach it in a whole new way.

Step 1: Focus on the lesson

Instead of beating yourself up, putting yourself down or punishing yourself, focus on what you can learn from the experience and how you can grow. Take a moment to look back at what happened with curiosity and openness. What would you like to learn from this experience? What can it teach you about who you would like to be and how you would like to live, going forward?

Ask yourself if there are any actions you might like to take now to correct things or make amends? If you caused someone pain, embarrassment or harm, in the spirit of honouring them, commit now to being a better version of yourself in future. Instead of punishing yourself, change, learn and grow from your mistakes for your own and everyone's benefit.

A wise teacher once said it to me, 'Regret is OK, but you only need a spoonful.' What he meant was that if we notice the mind going into regret mode, that's alright. It can be a great opportunity to recognise and honestly acknowledge that what we did was not helpful, skilful or kind for ourselves or others, and we can learn from it, making an intention to do better in the future. Let the mind take the lesson from what happened – that's what it wants.

This spoonful of regret really need not take long at all – maybe just a minute or so. It needs just enough time to acknowledge what happened, learn from it and grow. We can do it with an attitude of honouring any others involved as an act of love towards them and ourselves.

Step 2: Let the mind know that you have learned what you needed to learn and it's OK now to let it go

Remember that we can think of the mind as your inner guard dog, always trying to protect and serve you. In doing so, you might find it gravitates again and again towards replaying that mistake, regret or misfortune. Sometimes we need to communicate to the mind that we have already learned what we needed to learn and let it know that it can relax.

You can do this by saying to yourself in a warm and friendly tone, *Thanks, Mind, I've learned from this now. I got the lesson.* Then you can ground your attention in the moment and move on with the rest of your day with awareness. No matter how many times the mind tries to go back, just keep thanking it with patience and kindness. Keep reminding it that its work here is done: *Thanks, Mind, I got the lesson, buddy!* Then ground your attention back in the moment. It doesn't know any better than to play out its ancient conditioning, so we're retraining it to adopt healthier and more helpful ways to navigate life. By doing this, rather than being debilitating or unhelpful, our rumination, guilt and regrets can be great sources of wisdom, motivation, strength and mental clarity.

Remember compassion

When you find yourself overthinking, instead of judging yourself or becoming frustrated, try to treat yourself as you would a loved one who was distressed or in pain and adopt a kindly and compassionate attitude towards yourself and your mind. This will naturally begin to calm your nervous system, soothe your stress and clear your mind.

Summary

Our minds are capable of great things, but in this chapter, you have learned that in its effort to make sense of uncertainty and ensure our survival, your mind can get stuck in worry, rumination and other forms of overthinking. While these thought patterns were useful in ancient times to ensure our survival, these are habits that we need to break if we are to rise to our challenges constructively, take effective action and find peace, clarity and strength in the middle of it all.

In addition to the foundational tools from previous chapters, you have added an expansion to the Name It, Tame It, Reframe It practice to your toolbox. The two tools introduced here to specifically target over-thinking (constructive problem solving and 'Take the Lesson, Move On') will allow you to make good use of your mind's incredible abilities, adapting them so that, rather than dragging us below the mental strength line, they instead become helpful to us in times of challenge and struggle and shift us closer to a state of deep resilience.

8
Emotional Strength

Despite our best intentions, our highest hopes and our most dedicated efforts we will all, at some point, find ourselves face to face with emotional pain, distress and difficulty.

Loneliness, anger, fear and anxiety – they all eventually arrive at our door. It's simply not possible to avoid ever feeling bad – it's a natural part of human life – but we can learn to deal with emotional pain and distress in more healthy, helpful and empowering ways that lead us out of struggle, bolster our resilience and allow us to find peace in the midst of our pain. The key to achieving this is changing our relationship with emotional pain. Instead of reacting against it or succumbing to it, we can learn to see it and respond to it with awareness, equanimity, wisdom, skill and compassion.

In the book so far, you've learned several ways to develop mental strength by recognising and regulating your thoughts which naturally, in turn, impacts your emotional state. This chapter will help you focus more closely on working with and regulating your emotions so that you can harness their wisdom and regain your centre and strength in the middle of it all.

Fighting, fleeing and falling in

The prevailing wisdom of western culture says that when we are going through hard times, we should be stoic, think positively and use grit and sheer determination to push through and soldier on. Difficult feelings and vulnerability have no place at the table if we want to stay strong and deal with things successfully.

Parents, carers, managers and leaders can particularly feel the pressure to hold it together for everyone else. You're supposed to project confidence, always look calm, be able to handle it alone and shut down any fear or negativity bubbling up inside.

However, this goes against basic human biology. A healthy human being will likely have an influx of negative thoughts and feelings in response to uncertainty, grief, loss and distress. That could include feelings like anxiety, sadness, anger and fear and thoughts of worry, self-criticism, hostility, self-doubt, rumination and regret. That's just our minds and bodies doing the job they were designed to do: trying to solve problems, learn from the past, avoid potential dangers, anticipate and plan for the future and signal where we need to take action to stay safe and healthy. Our culture today seems to have bought into the philosophy that if it feels bad, we should get rid of it, get over it or, at the very least, hide it. The message is fed to us from a million different angles: feeling bad is bad.

In school, on TV, in workplaces and on social media we are continuously sent the message that normal emotions like sadness, fear, disappointment and anger are wrong, a mistake, flaw or failing or a sign that something is wrong with you or your life. Even if you're going through something tragic, incredibly difficult or intensely painful, the message is that these 'bad' emotions should be stopped or eliminated, or, even worse, that there is something wrong with you for having them.

We need to be clear: there is nothing wrong with having painful feelings. They are a natural part of the human experience and certainly a natural part of going through a difficult time.

When pain hits us, the mind's natural knee-jerk response is to want to get rid of or resist emotional pain with all its might. You might want to banish it, stamp on it, crush it, drown it out or do anything you can to get rid of it. What could be more understandable than our minds wanting to move us away from pain? What if, though, in an attempt to eliminate your distress in these ways, your mind was unknowingly creating far more of it instead?

Research shows that this is exactly what can happen. The amplification effect applies to emotions too: the more we try to numb them, drown them out, distract them and push them down, the louder they become and the longer they persist.[36]

The evidence also makes clear that if we ignore our feelings, try to get rid of them or stuff them down, we also miss out on valuable information about what's right, helpful and healthy for us. Our feelings are often signposts giving us guidance about how we can best navigate life and when and where we might need to make changes in our lives. Although they aren't pleasant, 'bad' feelings are often our greatest and most important guides and teachers because they hold valuable information about ourselves and how we are living our lives – about where our boundaries have been crossed, where someone's actions don't feel right for us, where we need to speak up, where something is out of alignment with our values or where we have unmet needs.

Acknowledging that difficult feelings are a natural part of everyone's life, it makes sense to ensure that we have the right approach to dealing with them in the best way possible. We'll never be able to find true resilience or live wholeheartedly and fully if we are exiled from, or enemies with, our own feelings.

Central to the Deep Resilience Method is the understanding that our feelings are not wrong; nor are they enemies. All feelings have their place and purpose in our lives. It's not about *not* having certain feelings; it's about changing your relationship with them.

Relief, inner peace and the ability to find our deepest resilience only come when we learn to relate to our emotions with understanding, awareness and compassion. They are not enemies that we need to fight or get rid of; they are allies that are a natural part of human life and that can guide us to valuable information. By changing our relationship with emotions like this, we end the battle with ourselves and make space for something greater, wiser and stronger to move through us.

The inner battle we can never win

When difficult emotions arise, we tend to tip into one of three typical knee-jerk responses: fighting, falling in or fleeing. The challenge is that when they become our default modes of dealing with emotional pain, it makes the pain worse: the more we revert to these patterns, the more we drain our vitality, increase our stress and get thrown into turmoil.

In my work as a coach and educator, I regularly see people stumble, struggle and become debilitated, not because they have unpleasant feelings – that's inevitable and natural – but because they get fused with them. This happens in one of three ways:

- They **fight** the feelings, treating them like enemies and struggling against them.
- They **fall in**, getting overtaken by the emotion. They become hooked and overwhelmed,

engulfed in stress, despair, depression or reactivity.

- They **flee** situations that bring those emotions to the surface, even when doing so goes against their core values and prevents them from moving towards meaningful goals and meeting important needs.

In each case, they are either paying too much attention to their internal chatter, becoming fused with unhelpful thoughts, or they are fused with the emotion itself, which saps their inner strength and vitality, resources that could be put to far better use.

Fighting

As Carl Jung is reputed to have said, 'What you resist not only persists, but will grow in size.' We often unquestioningly assume that force is our greatest strength when it comes to overcoming our inner struggles, but that is not the case.

I learned this in part from my little brother, Marty, who is now a gifted and sought-after psychotherapist, proud stepfather and happy, loving partner. His life, however, wasn't always that way. For many years he struggled with depression, and after an accident that hurt his back and put him out of work, things got much worse.

A sensitive soul with a big heart, he desperately wanted to meet a partner, build a career and do something meaningful in the world, so he kept trying with all his might to get back on track, squash the feelings down, push through it and stay positive. It seemed, however, that the harder he tried, the deeper, darker and harder to manage his depression became.

This went on for many years, endlessly repeating cycles of struggle, depression, numbing and hopelessness including periods of intense darkness and suicidal ideation (including several actual attempts) interspersed with brief periods of relief; and then the fight and the struggle began again. Round and round in cycles like this he went for many years.

Then, after one particularly rough battle and bout of depression, we were having lunch with a few friends and I looked over at Marty. His face was... beaming! This was a guy who had experienced a lot of social anxiety in situations like this, but today he suddenly seemed different. He looked relaxed, a soft smile resting on his face. I was so happy for him but also desperately curious. I wanted to know how he had broken through his anxiety and seemed to feel so calm.

'What's happening with you today?' I asked, 'You look different.'

'I gave up!' he said, smiling.

'You gave up what?' I inquired, slightly concerned.

'Trying to force my fear and depression away. I'm tired of it,' he said, 'so I stopped pushing and struggling and I'm practising being kinder to myself.'

I smiled and hugged him. I knew from my own first-hand experience that this insight could change everything. For Marty, this was the beginning of a profound time of transformation. It wasn't the end of his bouts of depression, but it was the end of his war with himself and his self-defeating way of relating to and managing his feelings. It was also the beginning of a new way of being. Over time, many of those difficult feelings did ease significantly but, more importantly, he pursued a fulfilling life despite them and he has continued to flourish over the years, all because he stopped fighting his emotions and found a new way to relate to them.

Struggling with or resisting difficult emotions often comes in the form of a spiral of unhelpful thoughts about our situation, much of which consists of resistance and ramps up our distress and suffering even more. Examples of these unhelpful spiralling thoughts include: *This isn't fair! What's wrong with me? This shouldn't be happening. Why me? I hate this! What did I do to deserve this? I can't cope with this.* As we know, adding mental resistance to existing emotional pain adds layers of suffering on top of what we're already going through, but it is such an easy habit to fall into, and to some degree most of us do in the face of hard times.

Learning how to disengage the fight response is something I always spend time on when working with clients because the benefits of transforming this one pattern are enormous.

Fighting can also take the form of:

- Trying to push away or deny our distress or discomfort; pretending it's not happening

- Bottling things up, also known as 'keeping a stiff upper lip' or 'getting on with the show' – people may say things like, 'You can't let it bother you,' or, 'Just get over it'

- Pushing through using sheer willpower

- Distracting ourselves or staying busy, perhaps by overworking or with excessive shopping, internet use or TV

- Denial – telling ourselves and others that we're fine, we don't have a problem, we don't need any support, assistance or time off

- Numbing the feelings with alcohol, food, drugs or other substances and/or behaviours

While understandable as an initial response and mostly not problematic in small doses, these 'solutions' do become problematic when they become our default way of dealing with difficult emotions. Not only do they often bring a host of additional fallout (such as wasted time and money, damaged relationships, poor work performance, harm to our health and so on), they are also ineffective because nothing has been done to resolve or ease the underlying cause of the pain or to acknowledge the information the emotion may be holding for us. Therefore, the emotion may linger and get louder over time.

Difficult emotions are a bit like quicksand: the more you struggle against them, the deeper you sink and the more stuck you become. It's a totally natural instinct to initially struggle when you fall into quick-sand, but it definitely isn't helpful. To get out, you have to take a moment to collect yourself and then do the *opposite* of what your instincts are screaming at you to do: to escape quicksand, you need to stop struggling, lay on your back, relax and let yourself float on the surface.

When we experience unpleasant emotions, we all have the same reflexive instinct to struggle with them, but all that does is make us even more stuck and fused with the emotion. We can even feel like we are drowning in it. Again, although this is a perfectly understandable initial response, it isn't helpful because the best way to free ourselves from difficult emotions is to collect ourselves (Recognise and Regulate Thoughts and Emotions), let go of the struggle, accept them and relax. Only then can we respond to what we're facing from a place of inner strength and clarity.

EXERCISE 10: Three-minute exercise: Pain without a story

Scan your body for any kind of slightly unpleasant sensation and tune in to it. It could be mild tiredness, a little hunger, a small pain or itch. For a few moments, just feel it with curiosity. Don't engage in thinking about it; just feel the sensations of it in your body.

Try this for sixty seconds.

Now take a minute to generate some thoughts about it: *Oh my god, this is horrible, so annoying; What's wrong with me?*; *Why am I itchy/tired/in pain?*; *Why won't this stupid pain go away?*; *I hate this feeling!* and so on.

Try this for around a minute.

What did you experience when you layered some resistance on top of the feeling?

Most people find that there is more tension, stress and a low mood. Did anything surprise you?

Now come back to the sensation again and this time see if you can allow it to just be, to feel it with no mental dialogue, just the raw sensation. Importantly, try to meet it with a sense of acceptance, making room for it in your experience. You don't have to like it, but simply let it be there.

Try this for about a minute.

What did you notice? Many people report that when they meet the emotion with awareness and acceptance, they get some relief from tension and stress and can relax a bit. Some feel a sense of inner peace, steadiness and calm behind or surrounding the unpleasant sensation. Don't worry if this wasn't your experience. Rest assured that with a bit of practice, you will start to access more of a sense of calm, groundedness and soothing, even as you feel painful emotions.

You can access a guided audio version of this meditation (as well as all the other meditations and some additional resources) at www.melliobrien.com/bookgifts

---

Emotions serve important psychological and physiological purposes. They provide you with valuable information about yourself and the things that are happening around you. They are like little inner messengers that communicate important updates that can inform decision-making processes and motivate action.

For example, anger can tell you that a boundary has been crossed or you need to stand up to someone or ask for change. Fear may be informing you of a threat to your safety or wellbeing. Sadness may be suggesting that you need some self-care or to seek comfort and support from others. Loneliness, a feeling more and more common these days, is often flagging up that you're in need of more connection (or better-quality connections) in your life.

While fighting feelings may temporarily suppress them and give short-term relief, in the longer term, emotions may 'fight back' against suppression in an attempt to get the message across. They keep coming back and getting louder, deeper, stickier. They may even become 'chronic' and start to stick around, perhaps as lingering stress, burnout, anxiety or even depression that never seems to leave your side.

What we often don't realise is that avoiding emotions also takes a lot of mental effort, and as the emotions grow louder and stronger, you have to increase your coping methods. This can become a slippery slope, pulling you into ever more dramatic, time-consuming and unhelpful coping behaviours. Eventually, you are left with only scraps of energy for the truly important things in your life such as your loved ones, your meaningful goals, your hobbies and your health and wellbeing. The mental fight to resist our emotions becomes more and more counterproductive and debilitating, but if we learn to listen to our emotions, honouring them and giving them space to be fully experienced, we can start to turn things around and find healing, greater freedom and peace of mind.

Falling in

Another typical response is 'falling in', where we are consumed, overwhelmed or totally overtaken by the difficult emotion.

If emotional pain was an ocean, 'fighting' would be thrashing around on the surface, expending a huge amount of energy and becoming more and more drained and distressed. 'Falling in' is like sinking or even drowning in it, becoming totally engulfed by the pain and unable to see beyond it.

Falling in often comes with feelings of helplessness and powerlessness about how to handle our distress. Other times we might feel like it takes control of us and we may behave reactively, perhaps lashing out or acting rashly.

What we often forget when falling in is that emotions are, as Susan David says, 'data not directives'.[37] In other words, they may hold valuable information but they are not orders, or the ultimate source of truth. While it's important to listen to them, you are free to respond to them in whatever way seems appropriate. It's equally important to regulate them and decide consciously, from a higher part of ourselves, what actions we would like to take in response. We don't have to mindlessly obey them or play them out. We can practise discernment and decide what is useful and helpful to listen to and what is not.

While fighting or falling in are separate and distinct modes of behaving in response to difficult emotions, it is also common to swing from one to the other in loops. For instance, after a period of total overwhelm (falling in), sometimes we then go into fighting the feeling, perhaps through tipping into mental resistance, emotional eating or self-medicating with substances like alcohol or drugs. This gives some relief for a while, but soon enough another cycle of feeling overtaken by the emotion (falling in) begins once again. In essence, we're just swinging from one state of fusion to the other. This can lock us into an ongoing cycle of overwhelm, disempowerment and distress – unless something interrupts the pattern.

Learning how to break the cycle is the work my clients do with me, and it is the work you are doing with this book.

Fleeing

Wanting to avoid situations where a difficult emotion might arise is totally understandable and not necessarily a problem unless it's life diminishing or getting in the way of following meaningful goals or living in alignment with your values.

Consider a client of mine, Stephanie, who wanted to become a manager in her firm but was constantly avoiding any situations where she would be expected to speak in front of a group. She didn't want to feel the anxiety that she experienced with public speaking so she went out of her way to avoid any scenario in which she might be called on to talk. This was holding her back and getting in the way of fulfilling her heart's desire – to become a leader and grow in her career.

Fleeing challenging situations and the difficult emotions they invoke may allow you to feel more comfortable temporarily, but it also leaves a deeper kind of emptiness in the long run. It's OK now and then, but not if it becomes an ongoing strategy to protect yourself from unpleasant feelings. It stagnates personal growth, diminishes potential and stops us from staying true to our values and fulfilling our heart's deepest desires and goals. Furthermore, it's a downward spiral: the more we allow emotions to dominate our behaviour and boss us around, the more fused we become and the greater power they (seem) to have over us over time.

Three steps to regulate difficult emotions

So-called 'negative' emotions exist to keep us safe. As we've learned, they are not our enemies but our allies. Nevertheless, when we are in deep emotional pain, sometimes it's hard to remember this when we find ourselves lost in the fog of thoughts, reactions and feelings that are swarming in our heads. In hard times we will all likely find ourselves face to face with some really strong painful emotions like fear, grief, rage or shame.

Label It, Love It, Listen to It is a three-step process that helps us to work with difficult emotions (Recognise and Regulate) in a healthy, helpful and effective way. It anchors us in a sense of safety, calm and soothing, and allows us to act intentionally and wisely. This practice is the most powerful tool I know for working with difficult emotions. It amalgamates research findings from multiple fields with the wisdom of spiritual traditions. It is accessible, reliable and effective, even in those moments when it's hard to ground yourself and you're feeling a lot of inner turmoil, overwhelm or confusion. It has helped me through some of the darkest moments of my own life.

The three steps are:

1. **Label It:** Defuse from the emotion by recognising it, naming it and dropping any resistance to it, allowing you to ground in mindful awareness.

2. **Love It:** Attend to the emotion and yourself with acceptance and compassion, soothing your nervous system, heart and mind.

3. **Listen to It:** Gently enquire into what the emotion may have to teach or show you. Take action to support yourself as needed.

Step 1: Label It

Labelling (otherwise known as naming) emotions is a powerful way to recognise and regulate them, as we have seen. It also helps you act more skilfully, staying non-reactive and more clear-headed so that you can make more rational and wise decisions. Research shows that giving your feelings a name (labelling them) deactivates the amygdala (the part of the brain that initiates your fight-and-flight stress response), and causes increased activity in the area associated with managing emotions, particularly negative ones (the right ventrolateral prefrontal cortex).[38] This suggests that naming emotions helps regulate the body's stress reaction, and also enhances the ability to manage emotions, particularly difficult ones, in ways that help us thrive.

When a client of mine is overwhelmed with difficult emotions, the first thing we tend to explore is where the feeling is located in their body. It's not the same for everyone, but we often find that anger, for example, is felt as tightness and tension in the jaw, neck and shoulders, rapid breathing and heat in the body. Sadness is felt as a heaviness in the chest or stomach and low energy. Shame may be experienced as an emptiness in the belly, and fear or anxiety as a churning in the stomach and waves of tingling energy throughout the body.

By tuning into the feelings and sensations with awareness and acceptance, we do two helpful things at once. First, we bring awareness back to the primary experience so that we can begin to defuse from any unhelpful thoughts which tend to arise in response to painful emotions. That helps us to find more inner calm, grounding and clarity and opens up more mental space. Second, we begin to break the cycle of fusion (fighting, fleeing or falling in) by gently turning towards the emotion instead of away from it.

Why would we want to turn towards an unpleasant feeling? A surprising and counterintuitive result of staying with something in this way, even when it feels uncomfortable, is that the instinctive urge to get rid of the feeling (by fighting, fleeing or falling in) lessens and sometimes even disappears, even while staying in contact with the emotion. A successful encounter of this type can sometimes unravel long-standing problematic coping patterns, offering a healthier relationship with unpleasant emotions in the future.

Turning towards difficult emotions or sensations in a way that is non-reactive, accepting and helpful also allows us to connect with mindful awareness, giving us the power to make more intentional choices, take wiser actions and attain greater inner equanimity.

'Labelling' is an umbrella term for turning towards an experience with awareness. Mental labelling requires us to fully recognise the emotion and involves deeper engagement with it. While it brings us closer to the experience of the emotion, which may seem counterintuitive, it's the necessary first step in defusing from the emotion and provides a bit of mental space and perspective.

We've already seen in Chapter 5 how the practice of mentally acknowledging unhelpful thoughts (by thanking the mind) can be a powerful way to defuse from unhelpful thinking patterns and open up to a greater awareness, especially when done with kindness and patience.

When something is troubling us and we're experiencing strong, charged and difficult emotions, the act of naming the emotions can help us step back (defuse) just enough to remain in contact with the feeling without getting stuck in patterns of fighting, fleeing or falling in. Mentally labelling when emotions are present – *Anger is here, I am feeling grief, Doubt is arising, This is confusion* – makes it easier for us to just be with the emotions without struggling and opens the way for us to find a more helpful path forward.

Sometimes we don't know or can't be clear what the specific emotion is that we're feeling at that moment. In that case, another option is just to practise labelling in a broader sense: *Ouch, this hurts!* or *This is a moment of pain.*

How we label an emotion is also important. We want to do it in a gentle way using a kindly and compassionate tone for your inner voice as you label. A Zen teacher once told me it should be soft – like a feather lightly touching a floating bubble. Just the gentlest of acknowledgements. If you find yourself barking at the emotion, you will increase inner tension and struggle and will probably find that underneath that aggression towards the emotion is resistance. This means that you're still in fusion, to some degree, and so you're still working with an agenda of trying to make the emotion go away, which is not what we are aiming to do here. Soft and gentle mental labelling helps the mind let go of any tendency to fuse and allows you to relax on the surface and catch your breath.

Part of the process of labelling an emotion is bringing that attitude of acceptance to yourself and the feelings or sensations you have; in other words, allowing them to be there, without trying to fix, avoid or fight against them. To assist this, people often find it helpful to use the mantra of inner peace: *It's OK for this to be here*, or *Right now it's like this*. Allowing an emotion doesn't mean you have to like it or want it. It just means accepting that it's already here and waging peace with it. By aiming to reduce your mental resistance to what is happening, you reduce the amount of additional suffering that is added on top.

When you allow strong emotions to be present, you may notice an almost immediate sense of softening and ease around the emotion. To circle back to the quicksand metaphor, this is the moment where you catch your breath and collect yourself, stop struggling or sinking, lay back and relax on top of the quicksand and float.

Step 2: Love It

The second step of the process is to bring a sense of nurturing and kindness to your emotions. Rather than shutting down or going into battle with ourselves when we're hurting or distressed, self-compassion soothes our body, calms and clears our mind and engages our innate wisdom. It brings peace to our pain.

Research shows that when we practise self-compassion, our body's threat response is down-regulated.[39] This has been associated with an increase in positive emotions (such as happiness, satisfaction, appreciation and optimism) and lower levels of stress, anxiety and depression.[40] In this calmer physiological and mental state, we're able to become less emotionally reactive and make more skilful choices about the best next steps to support ourselves through hard times.

Studies also suggest that people who cultivate compassion for themselves during difficult times have greater resilience to cope with stressful life events.[41] They also bounce back faster and experience greater life satisfaction over the long term than those who do not engage in self-compassion, and tend to experience less anxiety and depression.[42] In our darkest moments, it's important to remember that this is when we need acceptance, kindness and gentleness towards ourselves the most.

This step involves taking a moment to say to yourself, *May I be kind to myself in this moment*, or, another possible phrase that comes from Vietnamese monk, poet and peace activist Thich Nhat Hanh, 'Darling, I am here for you' (directed at the emotion itself).[43] As you say this, you might like to place a hand over your heart or make another gesture of self-compassion. See if you can bring an attitude of kindness and tenderness to yourself and your emotions even in the midst of your pain. In the meditations I do with my clients, we often linger on this step for some time. We use imagery, the breath or verbal mantras like the ones mentioned above to surround and cradle the pain in compassion, allowing resistance to soften and enabling them to become more at ease and accepting of what is.

In the face of strong emotional pain, practising kindness and compassion soothes the nervous system, brings us comfort and settles the mind. Bringing love to our pain creates some mental space around the fear, stress and anger so it is now surrounded by loving awareness, giving us back the capacity and composure to take wise and skilful action if needed.

Imagine putting a tablespoon of salt into a cup of water; that water will be intensely salty and unpleasant to taste. Now imagine if you put that same tablespoon of salt into a swimming pool of water; it will be barely perceptible.

In the same way, when experiencing strong emotions our mind tends to fixate on them and so they feel intense and overwhelming. They take up almost all our mental space. On the other hand, when we bring loving awareness to them, emotions are now held in a larger container of love, acceptance, understanding and kindness. Even though the emotion is still there, it suddenly doesn't seem to bother us in the same way and we don't take it so personally. As we connect to a deeper part of ourselves that is much vaster than the emotion, we gain a much greater perspective on what is happening in that moment.

Instead of trying to fix, change, eliminate, solve or struggle against difficult or painful emotions, we give them the love, comfort and attention they have been longing for. Giving the emotions this space to be held in paradoxically means that they are more likely to dissolve and pass in a healthy way as they are no longer being amplified through fusion.

**EXERCISE 11: Three-minute exercise:
A container of loving awareness**

Recall the last time you felt a difficult emotion of any kind. See if you can feel that same emotion in your body now. Try not to work with anything too overwhelming – lean towards something mild or medium on the range of emotions.

Got it?

For a few moments, just feel the sensation of the emotion with curiosity. Don't engage in thinking about it; simply feel it.

Whatever the feeling, see if you can create a safe space within you for this feeling to be held – a container of loving awareness that can hold whatever you are feeling in a gentle, compassionate and accepting way.

See if you can find a sense of tending to the pain, resistance or discomfort as you would a loved one who was hurting. If someone you cared about was in pain, you wouldn't try to make them go away or ignore them; you'd offer them support, a hug or simply a loving supportive presence to be alongside them in their experience.

Now see if you can meet your own difficult emotions in the same non-judgemental and compassionate way. Allow the emotions to arise, acknowledge them and create a safe container of awareness for them. Many people find it helpful to imagine breathing kindness and compassion right into where you feel the pain the most. You may also find it helpful to place your hand over the place where you feel the emotion.

Take a moment to notice that the deeper part of you, the container of awareness holding and observing the emotion, is not affected, changed or moved by anything happening within it. For instance, your awareness of anger isn't itself angry; your awareness of fear is not afraid; your awareness of sadness isn't sad. Connecting to this deeper part of yourself, you find greater freedom and peace in the middle of it all.

Try this practice now for two minutes, if it feels OK to do so.

You can access a guided audio version of this meditation (as well as all the other meditations and some additional resources) at www.melliobrien.com/bookgifts

---

Well done for giving that a try. What did you notice? Any sense of ease, relaxation or comfort? Many people find that this is the case but don't worry if you found it tricky. For many people, this way of being with our emotions is totally new. Rest assured that it gets easier over time and with practice.

When we create this container of awareness, we learn to offer a safe space for our emotions. A space for them to be held with compassion, wisdom, gentleness and acceptance. With this safe and strong capacity created within ourselves, we will find we can be with anything, no matter how hard or scary it feels.

It's normal to feel a little bit of discomfort when turning towards difficult emotions; however if, during the above practice, emotions start to feel too overwhelming to stay in touch with, you can also *turn away with awareness*. Instead of staying focused on turning towards the emotion, you can take your focus *away* from the pain to another object of attention, such as sounds, your breath or the feeling of your feet on the floor. Stay with that anchor for a while until you feel more comfortable, settled and grounded. Then, if it feels right, you can try again to use the steps, toggling back and forth as much as needed or, of course, you can stop and try again another time.

Step 3: Listen to It

It has been proposed by leading experts in the field of emotion that there are seven universal basic human emotions: sadness, happiness, surprise, fear, anger, disgust and contempt.[44] It is worth noting that out of these seven, five are associated with more difficult parts of the human experience. What does this say about us?

Firstly, it suggests that these emotions are a natural and normal part of the human experience and secondly, that they have a purpose. Psychologist and creator of non-violent communication Marshall

Rosenberg describes emotions as unique messengers that carry specific signals regarding our needs and values and whether or not they are being met or honoured.[45] Even though they can be unpleasant to experience, negative emotions are often powerful guides holding valuable information about what our needs are and where we need to make (or ask for) change, uphold boundaries, say no, take rest or reach out for support.

Sometimes the cause or source of the emotional pain is obvious and immediate: breakups, deaths, job losses and so on. Some painful emotions can also arise when life is out of balance, or in response to unmet needs such as a lack of connection with others, with nature or with meaningful work. It can also develop from unhelpful thinking and behavioural patterns, as we have seen.

By listening to our emotions and finding out what they may have to show us, we can start finding ways to address our unmet needs, reconnect to our values, unwind from the thoughts and behaviours that hinder our happiness and strength, and do the things that help us flourish. Our emotions can guide us home to our authentic and best selves and the life we want to live, like a wise friend who takes our hand and helps us find the path.

Now that you have labelled and loved this emotion, you are no longer locked into unhelpful and reactive patterns of fighting, falling in or fleeing, and you have connected to awareness and compassion, which means you are better able to respond. You are now at a point where you can choose to investigate your experience with care and curiosity. This is done by asking yourself questions mentally – and then listening to the answers. This process of enquiring into our emotions can help us unlock the wisdom they contain and also enables us to identify and defuse from mental/emotional/behavioural patterns that may be generating unnecessary suffering or distress. It helps us tease apart the causes and conditions that created the emotion and from there, we are well placed to take some positive next steps.

You may not always feel that you need this third step as sometimes just the recognition (Label It) and acceptance (Love It) of the emotion is enough; at other times, you may feel particularly drawn to using this additional step.

To listen, you can ask yourself questions like:

- *Why do I feel the way I do?*

- *Are there events that happened ahead of the emotion that might have influenced it?*

- *Are there physiological factors that are affecting the emotion?* This could include things such as physical pain, not getting enough sleep or rest, insufficient connection to others and so on.

- *What thoughts am I having that may be contributing to the way I feel?*

- *If this emotion had a voice, what would it say?*

- *Are there unmet needs that may be contributing to this feeling? If so, what are they?*

- *Are there actions I could take to nurture and support myself at this time?*

You may feel drawn to just one of these questions or you may like to ask yourself a couple or all of them. You can always create your own questions too. After you ask the question, have a sense of inner listening and see what answers come to you.

The act of investigating your emotions and listening to them may bring about some immediate resolve, which can, in turn, unwind or even dissolve the emotion (although this is not the goal). Other times, you may gain valuable insights and suggestions on how best to proceed. Whenever it is that you hear the emotion speaking, see if you can listen with an open, curious attitude.

After you complete the *Label it, Love it, Listen to It* practice, make an intention to proceed with your next activities with awareness and self-compassion. You may also feel inspired to take compassionate actions that are helpful and life affirming, despite feeling difficult emotions.

It might be something simple, like running yourself a bath to soothe yourself, calling a friend, taking action on a meaningful goal or having an important conversation with a friend to clear something up. It could just mean deciding to rest, to play or to cook a healthy meal. Whatever it is, you will be acting from a connectedness to wisdom, awareness and compassion.

We may not be in control of all our circumstances, all of our thoughts or the emotions that may arise in response to them, but we are still in control of the most important factors that determine our resilience, our fulfilment and our overall quality of life: our attitude towards those things and our actions in response to them. This is how our emotions can guide us home to our authentic selves, as Nhat Hanh explains: 'Your body needs you, your feelings need you, your perceptions need you. Your suffering needs you to acknowledge it. Go home and be there for all these things.'[46]

Summary

All emotions, even unpleasant ones, have a purpose and can be our allies in living a wise, effective and meaningful life. It's not a bad thing to have them, nor is there anything wrong with you for having them. They are not a sign of weakness. They are sign of being human, and they can be a great source of strength.

Although some emotions are painful, they can help us identify our needs and values and take action to meet them or to come into closer alignment with them. None of us wants to experience even minor discomfort, let alone tumultuous difficult emotions, but they inevitably will arise in the flow of our lives, over and over again. If we can recognise when we're falling into patterns of fighting, falling in and fleeing our difficult emotions, we can instead regulate those feelings and work with them more skilfully. Unpleasant as they are, they can help us find our deepest resilience, heal our suffering and connect us to peace, purpose and wisdom amid our pain.

9
Growing The Good

*T*he feeling of warm sun on my skin. The sound of the wind in the trees. The changing colours of the sky. The sound of the kookaburra's birdsong. The feeling of my breath.

Sue was a participant on a retreat that I was running and this list was part of her homework, completed while watching the sun rise over the hills in Byron Bay. After sitting there a little while longer, she walked slowly to breakfast, stopping occasionally to smell the flowers, basking in the warmth of the day soaking into her body. Sue had been here four days and she was doing something that for a long time she hadn't considered possible: she was enjoying her life again.

For many months prior, she had been grappling with ongoing depressive moods and anxiety after going through a divorce. She still felt the heavy ball of sadness in her stomach that had been there for months but at this moment, it didn't seem to be bothering her that much. Surrounding the familiar heaviness, there was now a growing sense of fulfilment and calm. She felt at peace with her sadness in the here and now and this allowed her to open herself up to life again.

By learning to recognise and regulate many of the emotional patterns that were pulling her into suffering, Sue had already gained a lot from the retreat. Now, however, she was learning something even more impactful: that she could still lead a fulfilling, wholehearted and meaningful life, even amid her struggles and pain. Of course, she preferred that her sadness would go away, but in the meantime, she could now see that it was still possible to find beauty, happiness and meaning even while it was still there. This realisation had brought her renewed vitality and inner strength.

We may stand in awe of those who manage to remain optimistic and maintain a strength of purpose in times of adversity, but it is not an ability possessed by only the rare few. Researchers have identified the specific patterns in the human mind that make it so easy to slip into pessimism and overwhelm and so hard to find pleasure and meaning in life when you're going through an uncertain, challenging or painful period of your life.[47] More importantly, it has also become clear how to break away from the dark sway of these patterns and instead open the door to a whole new dimension of resilience and wellbeing that stays with us no matter what we are going through. In this final chapter on the Recognise and Regulate step of the Deep Resilience Method you will learn how to do this too. I will show you that you don't have to wait for everything to be fixed, changed or resolved in your life before you allow yourself to feel happiness and embrace meaning and goodness in your life. The practices we introduce in this chapter will help you reconnect to peace and purpose right now, just as Sue did with the rising sun at her back.

The negativity bias

As we learned in the first chapter, an unfortunate side effect of thousands of years of evolution is that, because of the mind's survival-based conditioning, it can easily tip us into FEAR and cause us to suffer.

Our mind is our main survival tool. We don't have sharp teeth, long claws, incredible speed or strength like other animals. At first glance, you might wonder how we survived at all in the forests and savannahs of the ancient world, but survive we did and not only that, we thrived, to become the dominant species on the planet.

The reason for this was our incredible intellect. Able to cast itself into the future, and also learn from the past, our mind allowed us to solve complex problems and plan ahead to anticipate and avoid danger. It focused on rewards too, using its incredible capacities to increase quality of life and create comfort and pleasurable experiences. But more than anything, and with good reason, it focused on survival as the top priority. Because this is the top priority, our mind has a negativity bias that not only operated in our ancestors but continues within us today.

Negativity bias, also known as positive-negative asymmetry, is the tendency to give disproportionate thought, weight and consideration to negative events, information and experiences when compared to positive ones. It was helpful when our survival depended on the ability to pay attention and react to negative experiences quickly. Remember our Great-great-great-great-great-great-great-Auntie Mabel and the rainbow outside her cave? If she came out of her cave to see a rainbow on one side and a strange shadow on the other, her attention needs to go to the shadow... and fast. Her life depended on focusing on the negative first and fast.

Our brains have evolved to highlight negative experiences and potential problems, store them in our memory and keep focusing on them so that we are more likely to avoid potential threats in the future. 'The mind is like Velcro for bad experiences, and like Teflon for good experiences,' is how neuropsychologist and author Rick Hanson explains it.[48] That is, negative experiences tend to stick in the mind whereas good experiences slide away far more easily.

Most of us no longer live in a world of constant danger but our brain still operates as if we do. This means that, because of our negativity bias, we tend to:

- Stew and fixate on our problems and what is going wrong way more than on what is going right in our lives

- Recall insults better than compliments

- Focus on our flaws and failings more than our strengths (and those of other people)

- Remember painful or negative experiences better than positive ones

- Worry about what could go wrong more than we get excited about what could go right

- Perceive possible threats and problems everywhere

- Think about negative things more frequently than positive things

- Pay attention to, react to and get more impacted by negative events than by those that are equally positive

- Make decisions based more on negative information than on positive

As we know, when you're going through hard times, uncertain or painful situations, the mind tends to ramp up all that FEAR-based circuitry. This causes the negativity bias to kick into high gear.

This is why your mind zeroes in on all the difficulty, pain and suffering in your life, almost to the exclusion of everything else and focuses on the bad things in your life with laser-like sharpness. In doing this it also fades out all the good, pleasant and enjoyable things that are still there. It can feel like they've been muted in volume so that you can't *feel* the pleasure, joy and meaning from them anymore. As one of my clients said, 'Life just started to feel like cardboard. Just meh.'

The people who love you, the taste of your favourite tea, the hobby you used to love, the smile from the cashier at the store, the warmth and cosiness of your bed, the pretty sunsets, the melody of your favourite music that used to send shivers down your spine – they are often overlooked or drowned out as we home in on what's wrong or lacking. We can become blinded to all the light in our lives and in ourselves when we focus on the darkness, and this impacts how we feel and our quality of life.

While this bias towards the negative makes sense from an evolutionary perspective, it can make for a truly depressing and difficult existence. Over time, it takes a significant toll on your mental health, potentially causing you to:

- Dwell on dark thoughts

- Experience frequent low moods

- Damage your relationships with others

- Develop a pessimistic outlook on life

- Feel drained of energy, both mentally and physically

- Feel disempowered or like things are hopeless

- Become more bitter and resentful

- Give up on your hopes, dreams and goals

Research has shown that the negativity bias has a strong correlation with the development of anxiety and depression.[49]

The negativity bias worked well as a survival strategy for our ancestors: it was better to be pessimistic and stressed but alive than to be happy and then dead. These days, though, we want to do more than just survive; we want to thrive. That's why it's important to actively work to balance out the bias.

Having recognised the negativity bias, we are now ready to learn how to regulate it. In this final and critical part of the Recognise and Regulate step we will learn how to rewire this pattern so that it is no longer a source of struggle but instead becomes one of our greatest sources of strength.

As these inherited patterns begin to calm down, you will be able to see life more clearly, act more effectively and be less thrown around and impacted by the challenges and upsets of daily life. It will help you regain vitality and lift your mood, while also reducing your anxiety, stress, unhappiness and exhaustion. As you open up to new vistas of beauty, meaning and joy in your life you'll recharge your batteries, regain that sparkle in your eye and, over time, fall in love with life again.

In the Deep Resilience Method, we work on rebalancing and strengthening the mind against negativity bias using two key skills: Savouring and Service.

Savouring

Here is some great news: over time and with a bit of practice, we can balance out the negativity bias and even totally rewire our brains to see things in a more helpful and balanced way. As neuropsychologist Donald Hebb explained, 'neurons that fire together, wire together.'[50] In other words, we do not need to stay stuck in our current patterns of mind and we can change things for the better by practising helpful new skills. Just like learning to ride a bike, drive a car or type on a keyboard, with practice, patience and persistence these skills can become second nature.

This is not about wearing rose-coloured lenses – we're not just going to pretend that everything is wonderful and ignore the hard things. It's just about taking off the dark lenses so we can see life without an imposed negative skew. With a clearer and more balanced perspective, we will be able to better see and enjoy the beauty, pleasure and meaning in life, even when facing the hard and painful stuff. This rebalancing comes from deliberately bringing more awareness to what is already pleasurable and good in everyday life.

There is a powerful technique I'd like to share that can help you feel better and stronger and will also rewire your brain's neural pathways for the long term. Drawn from positive neuroplasticity training and techniques, it will help you to hardwire elevated and uplifting emotions in and balance out the negativity bias, helping you stay more resilient, energised and whole.

I call this technique Savouring. It has three simple steps:

1. Seek

2. Soak it in

3. Save

Step 1: Seek

Deliberately seek out and aim to notice good experiences each day. Pay attention to them instead of overlooking them. Pause to appreciate the beauty in your garden, the warmth of a hug, the comfort of your bed, the sweetness of an apple – notice all these little moments of pleasure, enjoyment and goodness in your life. We so often overlook all the abundance, kindness, love, safety, peace and beauty around us but by actively seeking them out, a process within your brain is activated and you will gradually start instinctively taking in more of the goodness and beauty already present in your life.

You can tune in to both pleasurable external experiences as well as internal experiences, such as when you feel joy, contentment, relaxation, courage, love or playfulness.

This is not a process of actively thinking about all the good things; it's about noticing and paying attention to them in your primary experience as you go about your day.

Step 2: Soak it in

Really open yourself up to the experience. Once you have noticed something pleasant or good, pause and let your full attention stay with the experience for at least five to ten seconds (this is how long you need for new neural pathways to set in). Open yourself up to the bodily sensations, emotions and all that is happening in the moment. Drink in the good experience fully, letting it fill your mind and body and see if you can deliberately build up the intensity of the good feelings.

As you do this, the experience will move from your short-term to your long-term memory, which is important for rewiring your brain to take in more good going forward so take your time to truly connect with these feelings. Allow the experience to sink deep into your being as you engage fully with it.

Remember, this is not about positive thinking; it is about you fully absorbing the direct sensory experience of what is happening.

Step 3: Save

Allow the experience to really sink in and become a part of you. Feel it settling deeply into your mind and body and set the intention to take it with you in memory and in your being. Say to yourself, *This goodness is with me now.*

If you find it helpful, you can take a moment to imagine absorbing a golden light or a jewel placed in a treasure chest stored deep within your heart. However you do it, just find a way to feel that you're taking this goodness with you in memory, in your body and in your being. It is a part of you now.

The more we seek, soak it in and save this type of experience, the more we will begin to see and experience life in a more balanced way. It's not that we ignore the negative experiences or stop difficult or unpleasant things from happening – they're a natural part of life – but we can make sure we're seeing things from a balanced perspective so that we don't become overwhelmed and dragged down by that negativity bias.

As you cultivate this capacity for taking in the goodness and pleasure around you, you'll notice a shift in your perceptions towards a more uplifting view of life. You'll likely also experience a new lightness and ease of heart and mind, and a little more joy and wonder flowing into your days.

Some people find that they have some internal resistance to focusing on the positive aspects of life; isn't it all just a bit too fluffy? Remember, however, that this is grounded in solid science: multiple researchers in various allied fields have demonstrated that negativity bias can tip us into greater suffering and distress. Learning to counter this inherent negativity bias will give you energy, endurance and grit as you navigate forward through the choppy waters of life. It will also help you support others as the light you find within yourself will shine on those around you.

Opening yourself to the fullness of life

The breakthroughs you have made in earlier chapters, through which you've learned to soften the struggle with your pain, laid the groundwork for being able to open yourself up more fully to pleasure and meaning. It can be tempting to just try to open up to pleasure while blocking out all the pain, but as Brené Brown observes, '[We] cannot selectively numb emotion. When we numb [painful feelings], we numb joy, we numb gratitude, we numb happiness.'[51] When you resist and try to block out difficult thoughts and emotions, you also dull and block your ability to feel the goodness of the pleasant, positive and beautiful things in your life too. Have you ever noticed, for example, how when you're numbing yourself to pain, you also feel much less emotion in response to a beautiful piece of music, a stunning view or even your loved ones? You become partially alive to it, or as one of my coaching clients once said, 'I feel like a zombie. Just "getting through" life, putting one foot in front of the other but not really living.'

Dulling and numbing our feelings does not make for a rewarding life, so it's important to learn to soften the struggle and resistance to your pain before then trying to become more sensitive and receptive to the enjoyable and beautiful aspects of life. By recognising and regulating using these steps, we will become more alive and more in touch with the full spectrum of the human experience and find more peace and presence in the middle of it all. We become more able to live wholeheartedly and fully, no matter what life throws our way.

EXERCISE 12: Three-minute practice: Savouring the good

Now is a good time to spend three minutes taking in the good, following the three steps of savouring:

1. **Seek out the good experience.** Can you find something about your present moment or experience that is enjoyable, pleasant or good? It may be something simple like the soft touch of fabric against your skin. Being warm enough or cool enough. The soft rhythm of your breath. A pleasant sound. It could be the absence of hunger or the comfort of your sitting position. It could also be the feeling of being safe right now where you are. No immediate threats or dangers are coming and you're secure. Make this pleasant experience the focus of your attention now.

2. **Soak it in.** Stay with the experience for at least five to ten seconds (more is better) and let it build in intensity. Really take in how good the experience feels, how pleasant it is. Lean into it and allow that good feeling to really wash through your being and build within you.

3. **Save it.** Absorb the experience and take it with you. Say to yourself, *This goodness is with me now. Visualise, if you find it helpful, a jewel or a light becoming a part of you from now on.*

You can access a guided audio version of this meditation (as well as all the other meditations and some additional resources) at www.melliobrien.com/bookgifts

It can be helpful to take some time out to think about what are some good elements of your daily life that you don't usually overlook. What is beautiful, pleasant or enjoyable that you can appreciate and savour as you go about your days? You might like to make a mental note of them or write them down.

Make an intention to regularly notice and seek out those good things. Seek them out, soak them in and then save those experiences, letting them become a part of you.

Service

A wise man once said to me that the secret to living is giving. One thing I know for sure is that service – the desire or decision to help others – is one of the most potent and indomitable sources of inner strength I have ever witnessed in all my days at this work. The courage, the love, the inner strength and the wisdom that people can source when they decide they will devote themselves to helping others or making the world a better place is incredible. People who have been through unbelievable hardships sometimes experience the most powerful transformations and profound spiritual growth during difficult times when they decide to devote themselves to helping, healing and protecting others. In doing this, what they've done is transmute their pain into purpose.

Many years ago, I was working on a weekend retreat teaching stress management, deep relaxation and mindfulness to people who were full-time carers for a family member or partner. This was a hugely needed skill as, according to research, being a full-time carer is one of the most stressful situations that people can find themselves in and many burn out, break down or become depressed.[52] There were several other coaches and speakers also leading the retreat, one of whom was teaching about resilience. She didn't have a published book or a big following, she was simply a lady devoted to helping others. I don't remember her name, but I will never forget her absolutely heart-wrenching and yet truly inspiring story.

She had been a happy wife and mother and had a fulfilling career, but she had lost her entire family suddenly in a tragic incident. Understandably, she had fallen into a deep, dark depression. Unable to work during this time, her career also ground to a halt. She had often thought about taking her own life during the months that followed, but a series of events made her resolve to turn her pain into purpose: she was going to find a way to become resilient so that she could be there for anyone else who had to go through an equally tragic and traumatic experience. She didn't want them to feel alone and wanted them to know that someone else had been through a life-changing trauma and had found a way to love life again so they could too.

As she told her story to us that day, she radiated compassion, warmth and courage. Her story of overcoming her pain and transmuting it into love and service moved me to tears and made me realise that we are all stronger than we think when we draw on the deepest resources within ourselves.

Hers is, however, not the only story like that. There are stories of people who were on the verge of suicide but who then vowed to devote their life to service and went on to live meaningful and inspiring lives; people who risked everything to spread kindness in the death camps of Nazi Germany; people who overcame cruel injustices and stood up for the values they believed in even at great risk to themselves. These people, and those like them, show us that even those who have gone through the most painful, horrendous experiences can transform, heal, find purpose and flourish.

Serving others builds mental resilience. According to research, altruistic people tend to be happier, less depressed and more resilient.[53] Giving has a boomerang effect, benefiting the recipient but also lighting up the mind of the giver with positive emotion and enhancing inner strength. You know that warm-all-over feeling you get by donating, volunteering or offering someone a sincere thank you? That glow is your brain's reaction to your own act of kindness. Researchers have studied how the brain responds to giving using functional magnetic resonance imaging (fMRI).[54] Your brain releases cortisol (the 'stress hormone') when you are anxious, stressed or scared. Kind acts towards others regulate cortisol production, reducing anxiety and stress and triggering the brain to release neurotransmitters and hormones associated with happiness, including dopamine and serotonin.[55]

Low levels of these can cause depression so regularly practising kindness can be a natural antidepressant, producing feelings of contentment and pleasure. Physical pain can also be reduced through altruistic acts. That's because endorphins, your body's natural painkiller, are often released when you show kindness.[56] It also increases self-esteem, improves mood and helps you stay healthier and live longer.[57]

Even the smallest act of service towards others will bring you a host of benefits, including helping you to:

- Manage stress

- Reduce your risk of developing depression

- Increase your resilience

- Feel happier

- Gain a sense of purpose

- Feel more energetic

- Build meaningful connection with others, thereby reducing loneliness

- Experience reduced levels of physical pain

Ideas for service

There are many ways that we can give to others. Here are a few ideas:

Acts of service: Volunteer in the community at a community garden, animal shelter, homeless refuge, nursing home, school or food bank. Do something nice for someone else, such as helping a neighbour or a family member, or calling on someone who may need some support or company.

Philanthropy: Monetary donations can range from rounding up a few cents to contribute to a local cause to a large financial gift or legacy. It can also be giving someone your time, your skills, your understanding, your patience and a listening ear. Give them your presence. Smile at a stranger or give a kind word to someone who looks like they're having a hard day.

Appreciation, kindness and gratitude: Appreciation can be expressed in ways that are silent or spoken. Focus on what you appreciate about others and express it to them in words or gestures. See their good qualities and reflect your acknowledgement of their goodness back to them.

Kind acts towards others can also be something seemingly small, like a friendly smile and wave after another car slowed down to make space for you in the traffic, or taking a moment to thank a passer-by who alerted you to your dropped phone. It could be acknowledging how thoughtful it was that your partner took out the garbage or sending a quick text of encouragement to a friend who is going for a big goal, letting them know you believe in them.

Pay attention to what's good in others and in yourself. Be a gift wherever you go. Look for ways to inject a little sunshine into people's lives. As you do this, let that feeling of appreciation and goodwill soak into your heart and warm you, and let them know, both in words and deeds, that you are truly grateful for them and see their goodness.

Summary

After completing this last chapter in the Recognise and Regulate step, you can now spot your negativity bias and see when it is colouring your perception in unhelpful ways.

You have learned two more ways to rebalance your mind: Savouring and Service. Practising the tools and techniques in this chapter each day will restore your ability to find goodness, beauty and meaning even in the face of the worst of circumstances, and you will continue to build the strength and resilience that will stand you in good stead when you need them most.

PART TWO
CULTIVATING WISDOM

10

Step 2: Inhabit The Present Moment

It's not easy living a human life and going through times of adversity and stress, but fortunately we have what it takes to stay strong. The innate human capacities of presence (inhabiting the present moment) and purpose (staying connected to our values) give us the ability to rise to our challenges. With these, we have everything we need to tap into an enormous reservoir of strength, peace and confidence.

We now have the right tools to Recognise and Regulate Thoughts and Emotions and therefore unwind the patterns that hold us back and diminish our resilience and harness the power of our mind and emotions to help us navigate life skilfully. In the next two chapters, we will unpack how to tap into our greatest inner strengths (Steps 2 and 3), before turning in the final chapter to learn how to bring it all together to take empowered action (Step 4). Once we work through the remaining three steps in turn, we will have everything we need to RISE in the face of fear and live from a place of strength instead of struggle, no matter what life throws our way.

Guided by wisdom instead of governed by fear

It has been said that there are only two basic motivating forces in life – love and fear.[58] One thing is for sure, our primal mind tends to default to the latter, especially in hard times. However, as we have also learned, it is possible to defuse from FEAR-based patterns. Now that our actions are no longer being unconsciously driven by fear, we can draw our strength from a deeper part of ourselves. We can now be guided by wisdom, strength and purpose instead of being governed by fear.

Many people have come to work with me after their lives have crumbled or fallen apart. Often they're feeling lost, vulnerable, in turmoil and overwhelmed by suffering and distress, but when I am able to help them recognise and regulate the FEAR-based patterns that have been governing their lives, they are freed to access their deeper nature and its innate unshakable strength. From that place of deeper strength, they begin to live. The way they treat themselves and others, the way they perceive and interact with the world, the choices they make, the way they handle difficult moments – everything begins to change.

When people become connected to this deeper awareness, they simultaneously connect to inner resources like peace, fulfilment, clarity, courage and wisdom. When these qualities rise to the foreground, people often discover that the feelings of fear, overwhelm and hopelessness start to fade into the background. They feel more empowered and at ease, and they become more confident and clearer about what is needed in their lives for them to grow and thrive. They are tapping into a deeper resilience.

Deep resilience, in its essence, is the ability to shift from being dominated and pushed around by FEAR-based mental/emotional/behavioural patterns that hold us back, drag us down, inhibit our potential and cause us and others suffering, to living more and more from strength, awareness and love.

Two kinds of intelligence

When we think about who we are as humans, we tend to think of ourselves as individuals moving about in the world. We might identify ourselves by our names, our roles, our status or achievements, our beliefs: 'I'm Mary. I'm a mom, an accountant, middle aged and a spiritual person,' and so on.

Seen from another perspective, though, human beings are not separate individuals, disconnected from the rest of the world. Rather, each of us is a living system, made up of different parts, and these different parts interact with each other and have their own kind of intelligence.

The Deep Resilience Method invites you to access and embody an aspect of yourself that I call your deep nature or deep self; another word for it is 'awareness'. It's the part of you that exists beneath thoughts and feelings, so it can step back, observe them and choose how to respond.

In everyday language, we talk mainly about 'the body', by which we mean our physical body, and 'the mind'. This is sometimes referred to by some teachers and traditions as 'the thinking mind', 'the human mind', or 'the ego'. It is the conditioned thinking mind that runs the survival-based patterns we've been learning about in this book. To circle back to the analogy of the ocean, the thinking mind, when compared to the depths of awareness, is like the small waves on the surface of who you are.

Your deeper nature is able to observe both your physical body and your mind, all thoughts and emotions; therefore, it is more fundamentally and essentially *you*. It is the deepest, the most core aspect of who you are.

The deep self *is* awareness, the part of you that is aware of everything else: aware of every feeling, every thought, and every perception that you ever experience in your life. All thoughts, feelings and perceptions arise, unfold and dissolve in awareness like waves coming and going on the surface of the ocean.

Some people on a personal development or spiritual path make their mind into an enemy to overcome, subdue or get control of. They may even want to 'destroy the ego' or get rid of certain parts of themselves. In my experience, this attitude sets up an inner battle with ourselves that aggravates the mind, brings tension and stress into our system and blocks our ability to wake up to our deeper nature and higher potential as human beings.

That's not what the Deep Resilience Method is about.

Deep resilience is an approach that befriends the mind, treating it, and all parts of our selves, with understanding, respect and care. The mind/ego is a useful, valuable and essential part of our human system; however, the deep resilience model asserts that the thinking mind should not be the lead of our system – we've seen what kinds of things can happen when it is. Deep resilience is the ability to access and then act from our deeper nature and let it lead our system. With the deep self as the guiding force, we are better able to live guided by awareness and in ways that align with our values. We're better able to live from love and wisdom, not from fusion and fear.

The thinking mind has gifts and has worked so hard to keep us safe. It is good at what we might call intellectual intelligence: logic, planning, problem solving, memorisation and setting goals. It is skilled at manipulating the outside world, utilising the external environment to stay safe, get resources, attract a mate, make things happen and to apply the lessons from the past to the present. As we have seen, however, it also has primal survival-based wiring, and if left in the lead and operating unchecked without wisdom, it will play out its conditioned patterns, often to the detriment of our wellbeing, happiness and over-all quality of life. This applies both individually and collectively.

One aspect of this is that the thinking mind just doesn't know how to make you truly happy. It may lead you towards pleasure, but it knows nothing about how to lead a meaningful, fulfilling life. This is because it only has survival-based logic and condi-tioning to follow.

It also lacks wisdom, which is a different kind of intelligence, as we shall see. The American author and blogger Mark Manson neatly described why a thinking mind alone (what he calls 'intelligence') is not enough: 'Wisdom without intelligence can still lead to a good, simple life. Intelligence without wis-dom is a special (and dangerous) form of stupidity.'[59] Training our mind to be deeply resilient involves tapping into our inherent wisdom, the intelligence of our deeper nature, while also still being able to heal, harmonise and harness the incredible gifts of the thinking mind.

Deep nature

One of the assertions of the Deep Resilience Method is that everyone has a deeper dimension of themselves beyond just the content of the conditioned mind. In essence, this deeper self is who we truly are, beyond or beneath our conditioned thinking mind and physi-cal body.

This deep self is inherent within each of us and can be viewed as our true nature, our seat of consciousness and a place of deep inner 'knowing'. Some refer to this aspect of our self as our spirit or spiritual aspect. It is the part of you that remains constant. No matter what is going on in the conditioned mind or the world, your deep self is always the same, and remains untouched by external influences or experiences, just as the depths of the ocean are unaffected by the waves on the surface.

The world's wisdom traditions have their own way of communicating this aspect of human nature. Some call it the 'true self' or 'higher self'. In Buddhism it's your Buddha nature; in Hinduism it's 'Self' (with a capital 'S') or *Atman*; some simply call it the soul. Whatever they name it, these and many other traditions and teachings all acknowledge the trifold nature of human beings: body, mind and spirit.

We have seen how our thinking mind is conditioned by primal patterns and personal conditioning. In contrast, awareness is unconditioned: it's unchanging, ever present and its qualities are always available. It's the silent consciousness within that can observe thoughts, emotions, behaviours and all other experiences. It is before and beneath them. Deeper than them.

This is not an abstract concept but one that can be accessed first-hand fairly easily via a short meditation. You can take a moment to notice that a deeper part of you can observe thoughts and feelings rather than being caught up in them.

Various current cutting-edge evidence-based psychotherapeutic frameworks acknowledge and utilise this deeper part of human nature (along with other complementary skills) to help people overcome all kinds of mental struggles, find healing, make positive changes and drive personal growth.[60] Modern mindfulness training, which has proven incredibly effective in reducing stress, anxiety, depression and addiction and improving overall mental health, also cultivates and utilises this deeper awareness.[61]

The seven strengths of the deep self

Awareness is not just a blank slate of nothingness. It has its own kind of intelligence, which we can term 'wisdom', and is an enormous reservoir of inner strength, calm and wholeness. In my work with people over the years I have come to see that our deeper self has seven distinct qualities: love, clarity, peace, playful curiosity, courage, fulfilment and connection.

When combined, these qualities are what I would call wisdom, or what I sometimes refer to as spiritual intelligence – a way of being in the world guided by the aspects of our deeper being.

Over the years of working with many different people in workshops, retreats and in one-on-one coaching, I have found that, no matter what difficulties or mental struggles we were working with at the time, when I can guide them out of fusion and into a place of deep presence, by inhabiting the present moment, clients start to show these qualities.

1. **Love:** The most prominent of all the seven strengths is that of love. I have found that when they became connected to their deep nature, clients often understood things differently and began spontaneously showing compassion, care and kindness to both themselves and others. This often extended to feelings of benevolence, warmth and friendliness towards all of life. This love for life was often the catalyst for a change in living that reflected this new perspective on, and relationship with, the world around them. This aspect of our deeper awareness has been beautifully expressed by mindfulness teacher and author Mark Coleman: 'Do not tell me that kindness and awareness are different. Awareness is the foundation of kindness. Kindness is the expression of awareness.'[62]

2. **Clarity:** Once they inhabited the present moment deeply, people seemed to naturally connect to deeper insights and higher perspectives than were available to them before. Many had the sudden sense of confidence that they knew what to do in their lives and how to heal or manage certain internal and external struggles they had been grappling with. The problems and inner turmoil that had before seemed all consuming now suddenly felt manageable. No longer feeling

stuck, overwhelmed or confused, their minds calmed and cleared.

3. **Peace:** With enough defusion from FEAR, clients started to feel much greater inner peace. This often came with a sense of 'snapping out of it', waking up and finding a quiet and still place inside where they knew everything was fundamentally OK. I often saw an immediate change in their facial expressions when they touched down in this place of inner calm.

4. **Playful curiosity:** There was often quite a notable switch as they moved from being stuck in cycles of self-judgement, rigidity or resistance to a non-judgemental curiosity about different aspects of their experience, including difficult thoughts and feelings. Often they started displaying a more relaxed and open-hearted attitude towards themselves and their circumstances. This, in turn, softened and eased their minds and bodies and opened up more creativity and flexibility in their responses. They also showed greater cheerfulness and sometimes even a sense of humour about their situation for, as Eckhart Tolle observes: 'Life isn't as serious as the mind makes it out to be.'[63]

5. **Courage:** When inhabiting the present moment deeply, and connected to awareness, people often felt a shift to a sense of courage and confidence that they could handle whatever life might throw their way, and suddenly felt that they had all the resources inside to do so. They were better able

to stay brave in the face of fear, difficult emotions and thoughts, more able now to stand up to them and work with them skilfully. They also showed a firm commitment to their values and doing what they felt deep in their heart was right, even if it wasn't the smooth or easy option. This courage also allowed them to be more authentic in their expression of who they truly were, no longer so dominated by worry about what others would think.

6. **Fulfilment:** Connected with their deepest self, people found a new kind of contentment. They reported feeling connection to a sense of wholeness, completeness and fulfilment that wasn't dependent on anything external, and they often experienced feelings of profound wellbeing, along with gratitude for things that before had been overlooked.

7. **Connection:** People often reported a feeling of connection to something larger than themselves. Sometimes this was a feeling of spiritual connection, sometimes a greater sense of connection to people, the planet or even to life itself. With this sense of connection, they gained a much broader perspective on life, beyond their everyday circumstances. This in turn led to feelings of belonging, wholeness and even an enhanced reverence for life. Suddenly their problems felt smaller and more manageable in the context of a much broader and larger world view.

These qualities are inherent to our deeper nature so we have access to them in any given moment. They don't need to be created, built or manufactured. They simply need to be accessed. The ability to access and act from these strengths is what we might call wisdom or spiritual intelligence.

In this second step of the RISE framework, Inhabit the Present Moment, we focus on cultivating the skills to access and act from the strengths inherent in the deeper self again and again until they become more and more embodied and sink into our bones and our whole being like warm sunshine. They then flow out into the world through our speech, actions and attitudes.

Although words are tricky when it comes to our deep nature and ultimately fail to describe and define it, this transcendent part of our human nature is key in our journey to true, lasting and stable inner strength.

How to Inhabit the Present Moment

So far in this book we've covered why the human mind is a double-edged sword, and you've learned why your mind does what it does: that it is a survival machine trying to keep you safe, but that its programming is not helpful a lot of the time. We did not choose to have this tricky human mind, nor did we choose any of the adverse life experiences that have caused us pain and shaped us. However, we can choose how we respond to where we find ourselves now. We have the choice to respond to our circumstances from a place of strength.

We've already introduced mindfulness and have used it several ways in the Recognise and Regulate step to change our relationship to our thoughts and emotions. We now move on to Step 2: Inhabit the Present Moment; these first two steps are intertwined and in many ways inseparable from each other, but as part of this second step, we will learn to extend our capacity for mindfulness and tap into its gifts beyond what we have already learned.

Mindfulness is crucial to becoming deeply resilient. In fact, it's the foundational skill upon which every other step in the Deep Resilience Method depends, as without awareness we cannot step back, train or change the mind.

The Deep Resilience Method breaks mindfulness skills into three main categories:

1. **Grounding:** Grounding practices emphasise defusion. As we've learned, these are ways to unhook from, let go of, stop struggling against or step back from unhelpful thoughts and feelings and relate to them more skilfully. Grounding practices also help us embody more helpful attitudes such as acceptance, openness, curiosity and flexibility towards our experiences. They help us wake up out of FEAR, and often give us a sense of calm and stability.

2. **Connecting:** These are practices that place emphasis on connecting us to the present moment. They help us make contact with our primary experience and sense perceptions, which in turn helps us maintain mindful awareness.

3. **Resourcing:** These are practices that focus on accessing our deeper nature and its innate strengths. Resourcing also includes practices that help us connect with the seven strengths of the deep self and/or our values.

Mindfulness and meditation in daily life

Mindfulness

Mindfulness is a special type of awareness that can keep us anchored safely in the present moment and in our primary experience when the going gets tough. It is the practice of paying attention, without judgement, to the present moment as we experience it.

When thoughts and feelings are racing and swirling around in our heads, mindfulness helps us find our centre and tap into wisdom and strength, and eases our suffering. When we are mindful, there's no need to struggle with our experience because we have breathing room around it.

Mindfulness really has to be experienced directly to be truly known. It can't be expressed adequately in words. It is a preverbal way of encountering the world and it's something that we do all the time naturally, but we rarely pay attention to it.

You may have experienced moments of mindfulness spontaneously when watching the sun rising or setting, when listening to a beautiful piece of music, when making love or when fully engaged in a sport or some other activity you love. You may have become completely and utterly absorbed in the moment-to-moment experience, letting go of all the mental commentary, including your worries and plans, and just experienced the full vibrancy, freshness and fullness of life within and all around you. As you let go of wanting to fix or change things, you may have found yourself more able to open up and receive life just as it is.

While some people seem to be more naturally mindful than others (there is such a thing as trait mindfulness),[64] most people who are very mindful are that way simply because they practise it a lot. Just as exercise increases physical fitness, more mindfulness practice increases mental fitness in the form of being more aware in daily life. We can all increase our capacity for mindfulness through practice, no matter where we're starting from. You don't need to be a poet, monk or mystic. Everyone can access mindfulness – it's an innate human capacity.

EXERCISE 13: Five-minute mindfulness exercise: The song of this moment

Find a comfortable place to sit where you won't be disturbed and close your eyes if that feels OK for you.

Allow your attention to become like a radar, scanning your environment and picking up any sounds. See if you can let go of any judgement or mental commentary about the sounds and just listen to the sounds themselves. Receive them one by one as they arise and disappear.

See if you can take in not just the obvious sounds but also those that are more subtle. Try to find the sounds within the sounds. You don't need to listen to any particular sound – just receive the whole soundscape as it continues to change and unfold.

When you notice your mind has wandered away from listening to sounds, which it will likely do, lovingly return to the task of listening to the sounds that surround you in the moment.

Do this for five minutes with an awareness that this is the song of this particular moment in time. It will never be heard again. It is unique, fleeting and precious.

You can access a guided audio version of this meditation (as well as all the other meditations and some additional resources) at www.melliobrien.com/bookgifts

---

In the above exercise, as you listened with aware-ness, this was a moment of mindfulness. Each time you noticed your mind had wandered and you deliberately brought it back, this was also a moment of mindfulness. It's our ability to be present in the moment and bring ourselves back to the present moment each time we get lost in thinking. It's really that simple.

Cultivating mindfulness during meditation is a wonderful way to strengthen your mindfulness muscle.

Meditation

Meditation is the most common training ground for cultivating our ability to access and inhabit the present moment in daily life. It is what we could call the formal practice of mindfulness: time dedicated to the specific purpose of practising mindfulness.

We meditate to become familiar with, and more stable in, mindful awareness. This stability of awareness enables us to more easily access and embody the qualities of the deep self and become more adept at defusing from unhelpful thoughts. At first, we may only be able to sustain mindfulness for a short period, but over time and with regular practice, mindfulness helps us develop the ability to be more present throughout the day, every day. A good analogy for this is if you imagine taking a tub full of gold dye and dipping a white cloth into it. Do it once and the cloth will retain a little shimmer but most of the dye will run off. Dip the cloth in over and over, and each time more of the gold will soak in, until finally the cloth will appear fully gold.

When you practise embodying mindful awareness, you are steeping yourself in the wisdom of your deeper nature. This means that you can more easily call on it when you need it and it will more often guide your actions, thoughts and decisions. Despite some common misconceptions, this doesn't mean you'll be in an endless state of bliss or never make any mistakes, that you'll have no flaws or never feel pain again. Life will still sometimes be messy and hard, and other times beautiful, fun and pleasant. It simply means you're better able to meet it all from a place of greater wisdom, intention and awareness.

Meditation is not the only way to practise mindfulness, as we have seen. There are other options including yoga, breathwork, Qigong, t'ai chi and more.

Each person should decide for themselves whether it makes sense to establish a daily meditation practice. In my experience, meditation practice generally transforms the mind at a deep level, and often quite rapidly. It yields insights into our true nature, the workings of the mind and our personal conditioning. That can be deeply and profoundly liberating.

If you do wish to start daily meditation, be sure that your practice fits in with your temperament and lifestyle and be realistic with yourself so that you can stay consistent for long enough to really feel the transformational effects – I would suggest this needs at least eight weeks. It's better to start with shorter sessions practised consistently than doing one long practice every now and then. There are many ways to meditate, so explore what is right for you, but as a general guide, starting with fifteen minutes a day and then building to thirty to forty-five minutes a day will yield significant results and help you stabilise in connection to your deeper nature.

Meditation is never an end in itself, because life itself is always the real practice. It can be hard to stay grounded and aware amidst the flood of thoughts and emotions and challenges that we encounter in daily life.

Maintaining the ability to step out of fusion, let go of stress and respond to challenges wisely and effectively is a skill that will grow with every meditation practice.

Six simple ways to Inhabit the Present Moment

Apart from meditation, we can also tap into mindfulness at any given time throughout the day. You can use the following simple techniques to do so.

These practices are especially helpful any time we feel caught up, stressed, overwhelmed or in need of greater inner strength; we can use them to anchor ourselves in the present moment by reconnecting to our primary experience.

Take five deep breaths

This is a simple exercise to find your centre and connect with your deeper nature. You can do this anywhere and at any time, but it is especially useful if you find yourself feeling stressed or wanting to step out of reactivity and back into response mode.

Take a moment to focus your attention on your body and the sensations of your breathing. Focus on breathing in and out slowly but comfortably and with as much awareness as possible. Let everything else go for a few moments. Notice your body swelling and subsiding. Stay focused on one breath at a time – in and out, in and out. Count to five breaths.

Let go of tension

Deliberately scan your body for any tension, tightness, holding on or gripping. As you breathe out, deliberately soften and relax those areas of the body. You can start with one place, like the jaw. With the next breath soften the shoulders, then the belly, then the hands. You can keep doing this for up to ten breaths.

Zoom out

This exercise will help you to unhook from thoughts and connect with the world around you. It's especially helpful if the mind feels tense, constricted or fixated on a particular problem or worry.

'Zoom' your attention out from your thoughts, out from inside your head and into the world around you. Connect with your whole visual field. Look up and look around the whole room or out to the horizon if you can see it. Take in your whole experience, noticing what you can see, hear, smell, touch and feel. Absorb the whole world around you and let the moment in, like receiving a gift.

A sacred pause

Next time you feel reactive, rushed or overwhelmed, if things are difficult, if you are engaged in conflict or if you simply want to connect to a deeper awareness, physically stop what you're doing for at least five seconds (but up to a minute) and connect with the present moment. Tune in to your sense perceptions. Physically stopping whatever it is that you're doing sends a strong signal to your body and mind to shift gears. It interrupts our unconscious patterns and gives us a chance to catch our breath.

Drop anchor

Your feet are the farthest thing from your head so sometimes, when we are caught up in thinking, a helpful practice is to drop our attention down into our feet. Feel the sensations of your feet on the floor. Notice how they are connected to the ground and feel the solidity and stability of the earth beneath you. If you find it helpful, you can push your feet down into the ground or gently rock side to side to increase the feeling of contact. Notice the sensations as you do: tingling, pulsing, pressure, the touch of fabric against skin (if you have socks on, or are standing on carpet), the temperature, the feeling of the floor beneath you. Do this for as little as five seconds or as long as a minute.

Let go of time

One of the simplest ways to be mindful is to let go of thinking about the past and future and focus exclusively on the present moment. Remember that you only ever have to deal with one moment at a time. Be present for the one you're in. Let everything else go for a while and just focus on one thing, one moment at a time.

**EXERCISE 14: Five-minute mindfulness exercise:
Riding the waves of the breath**

Find a comfortable place to sit where you won't be
disturbed and close your eyes.

Take three slow deep full breaths in and out and, as you
do, tune your attention into feeling the sensations of
the breath moving in your body. You may like to focus
on the belly or the whole torso. Just feel the breath
wherever it's easiest for you to follow.

After three deep breaths, let your breath flow naturally,
letting go of all efforts to control it in any way. Continue
to follow the breath, allowing your attention to ride the
waves of the sensations of the breath as they move
through your body.

Do this for five minutes, staying in touch, as best you can,
with each wave of the breath as it rises and then passes.

Any time you notice that your mind has wandered away
from the breath, which it will likely do, with an attitude
of kindness and patience return your attention to the
feeling of the breath.

*You can access a guided audio version of this meditation
(as well as all the other meditations and some additional
resources) at* www.melliobrien.com/bookgifts

Inherent strength

One of the biggest misconceptions about deep resilience is that it is a self-improvement project, but deep

resilience is not about changing, improving or fixing yourself; it's about knowing yourself deeply and being yourself fully.

Because strength is who you are. Wisdom is who you are. Love is who you are. Peace is who you are. Wholeness is who you are.

Just pause and let that land for a moment.

You don't need to be fixed or improved. These qualities of our deeper being are always there within us and do not need to be created or developed, just accessed. We are practising not getting so caught up in the surface waves of the mind and learning to touch down on what is already and always there – a deep reservoir of wholeness, goodness and strength – and then seeing how much we can embody our deeper nature in our daily life.

To do this, it's really helpful to adopt this way of relating to ourselves as a system that you are the caretaker of. Your system has various parts: a body, a conditioned survival-machine mind and an unconditioned, unchanging, deeper nature containing wisdom. The more we, as the deep self, can learn to be the leader and caretaker of our system, the less we suffer and the more we can live from wisdom. Fear, stress, insecurity, anxiety and negativity cannot dominate when we're firmly rooted in our deeper nature.

You can cultivate wisdom by:

- **Inhabiting the present moment as much as you can**, thereby breaking fusion with FEAR and cultivating a stronger connection with the deep self. Practising meditation and mindful living will lay a strong foundation.

- **Deliberately and regularly connecting to and acting out the seven strengths.** Connecting can be done through practices that allow you to feel, cultivate and strengthen the states of being, the qualities and the emotions associated with the seven strengths. You can grow those strengths inside you through the upcoming anchoring practice and others. Acting them out involves living your daily life in a way that aligns with those strengths.

- **Staying connected to and living according to your own values** (more to come on values in the next chapter).

The wisest person you know

When clients tell me they're worried that they won't be able to or cannot connect to their deeper nature and its strengths, I always reassure them that it's much more accessible than we sometimes think. I ask them to imagine the wisest, kindest, strongest person they can imagine, someone who knows them really well (this can be an imaginary person or someone they might remember from their life). With this person in mind, I invite them to 'slow things down, take a few mindful breaths and tell me: what would that person say about your current situation or concern? What advice would they give you? What would they say to you right now?'

I am often amazed at how with just this simple prompt, I will often see a change come over people as they suddenly realise they already possess much more wisdom and clarity on what they're going through than they first thought. It gives them a doorway to access their own inherent wisdom and strength. You can try using this prompt any time you think it might be helpful in the flow of your life.

Letters from Love

Author and spiritual teacher Elizabeth Gilbert has been writing a letter to herself every day for over twenty-five years.[65] These letters are called 'Letters from Love' and the question Liz asks herself at the top of her journal is: 'Dear Love – What would you have me know today?' Then she puts pen to paper, writes from a place of awareness and Love speaks.

I have used this practice myself as a means of connecting to the energy of my deep self, and let me tell you, Love had a few things to say to me! Love told me many inconvenient things I didn't want to hear, notably repeating the all-too-familiar message that sometimes I need to slow down (I'm still working on it). Love has also told me about my own need to wake up. It kindly pointed out my blind spots and flaws, even as it surrounded me with compassion and encouraged me to greater authenticity, kindness and wisdom. It taught me humility. Love let me grieve the state of the world in a healthier way than I used to and helped me find the courage to keep fighting for what I believe in. It allowed me to trust life, trust our deeper nature and trust myself. Love encouraged me to keep teaching and writing even when I felt so inadequate to be the messenger for this kind of work. Most of all, Love kept reminding me that life is a miracle, that all life on this planet is my family and that every day is a gift. Many days, Love said, 'Just be kind, be present, be brave, and the rest will take care of itself.'

If this practice sounds like it may be helpful for you, give it a try. Try Gilbert's opening question or you could use your own journal prompts. You might find that Love, or your deep nature, has a few things to tell you too.

The Anchor of Strength

In my coaching and training sessions, we often use a powerful practice called the Anchor of Strength, which allows you to connect both with mindful awareness and with the strengths of the deep self. This meditation is a stand-out favourite of my clients and many of them report significant quick but enduring changes in their state of being, outlook and sense of empowerment.

The mind's tendency to tip into FEAR in hard times can be strong, and for many of us, it all too easily becomes our emotional and mental home, but we can create an anchor to something stronger. We can root ourselves in a place within our own being that is free of fear, a place of wholeness, peace and the deepest resilience. We can come home to ourselves and live in and from that strength.

In this exercise, we combine the principles of positive neuroplasticity training, mindfulness, neuro-linguistic programming and resourcing mindfulness techniques (techniques that focus on cultivating elevated and empowering states and internal strengths) to access and anchor ourselves to the wisdom of our deeper being. We also start to galvanise our access to the seven strengths so that they become a familiar place to land and live, easily accessible with just a gentle squeeze of your fist.

EXERCISE 15: Ten-minute practice: The Anchor of Strength

Start by finding your way into your meditation posture and when you're ready, gently close your eyes.

Begin with a minute of mindfulness, just following the flow of your breath and inhabiting the present moment more and more deeply.

When you are ready, bring to mind a feeling of **peace**. You might like to recall particular occasions when you felt calm, safe, at ease and relaxed. Perhaps you were standing at the ocean's edge or watching a sunset or sunrise. You can remember those moments or you can simply invoke the feeling of peace within you. Let it wash through you and come alive in you. Let it move through you, soothe you and ground you. What does peace feel like in your body? Intensify it. Let it build in you. That feeling when you know everything is OK.

Notice how you feel in your body when you're feeling peaceful. How you breathe and how you hold your body, feeling the calm, the serenity, the ease.

Bathe in that feeling, feel the goodness of it – the strength of it. Squeeze your right fist as you feel that peace, and then make an intention to take this feeling of peace forward in your life, saying to yourself, *This peace is with me now.*

Now let that feeling go and connect to a feeling of **clarity**, imagining or remembering a time when it felt like the mind cleared and calmed and you connected to a stillness, a deeper wisdom, a higher intelligence within you. Remember or imagine what it would feel like. Breathe how you breathe when you feel that kind of clarity; feel it in your body, that sensation when you connect to a deeper way of knowing and deeper way of understanding life, yourself and everyone – when you see things from a higher perspective. Feel the goodness of it – the strength of it.

Let this feeling of clarity flood through your body and squeeze your right fist as you feel it. Make an intention to take this clarity with you forward in your life – *This clarity is with me now.*

Now bring to mind a feeling of **playful curiosity**. Do you remember a time, maybe as a child, when you were open-hearted, curious and had a sense of wonder about the world around you? Think of some moments when you suddenly realised that life isn't always as serious as the mind makes it out to be. Bring that feeling to mind or imagine it, letting go of judgement or resistance and opening your heart to life.

What does it feel like in your body? How do you breathe? How do you hold yourself when you feel playful and curious? Intensify this feeling and bathe in this playful curiosity for at least a few breaths, feeling the goodness of it, the strength of it. Gently squeeze your right fist as you feel it, and then make an intention that you're now taking this quality with you forward in your life, saying to yourself, *Thank you, this playful curiosity is with me now.*

Bring **love** to mind now. Deliberately recall a time when you opened your heart to someone, when you were kind, when you gave someone the benefit of the doubt, when you forgave, or moments when you showed compassion or unconditional love. Imagine or remember love. Connect with it now, or generate it in your own way. Let it wash through you and come alive in you. Let it fill every cell, every sinew, every fibre of your being. What does love feel like in your body? In your mind and heart?

Bathe in that feeling, feel the goodness of it – the strength of it. Squeeze your right fist as you feel it, saying to yourself, *This love is with me now* as you feel it become a part of you.

Now connect to **courage**. Remember what courage feels like in your body as you recall moments when you were brave. The times when you faced hard things, when you stood up to fear, when you remained firm in your conviction to do what was right even when it wasn't easy. Maybe it was saying sorry, or facing something about yourself that was hard to see. Perhaps it was following your heart even when you feared rejection.

Remember or imagine that feeling and let it fill your body. You're resourceful, determined, confident, authentic, even playful when facing difficulty. You're empowered, you're focused on where you're going, on what matters deep in your heart, on your values, your purpose and your truth.

Let the feeling of courage fill your body. Soak it in. Squeeze your right fist as you feel it, saying to yourself, *This courage is with me now* as it becomes a part of you.

Bring to mind the feeling of **fulfilment**, a time when you felt whole, complete and content. Maybe it was a moment when you let go of wanting more, you stopped thinking about what you lack and instead shifted to a sense of appreciation. Maybe you were lying in bed on a Sunday morning totally relaxed and happy, or perhaps watching a sunrise? Maybe it was a moment when you realised what a miracle life is, and for that moment, you felt totally content, totally fulfilled.

Remember that feeling (or generate it) and connect with it deeply. Intensify the feeling and let it fill you up like warm sunshine. Feel the goodness of it, the strength of it. Squeeze your right fist, saying to yourself, *This fulfilment is with me now.*

Now bring to mind a feeling of **connection** – that feeling of being a part of something larger than yourself. This might have been a moment when you felt a spiritual connection or an awareness of your interconnectedness with others, the planet and all life. Perhaps you were looking up at the stars at night or you touched this connection in yoga, meditation or in nature. Remember or generate that sense of being connected, of belonging within the web of life, or belonging within the community, family or nature. Connect to a sense of oneness with it.

Let it wash through you and come alive in you. What does connection and belonging feel like in your body? Bathe in that feeling, feel the goodness of it, the strength of it. Squeeze your right fist as you feel it, and

then make an intention to take it forward in your life –
This connection is with me now.

Now reconnect with your breath and spend one minute
following the feeling of the breath as it moves through
your body.

When you are ready, open your eyes again.

*You can access this abridged version of the full meditation
(as well as all the other meditations and some additional
resources) at* www.melliobrien.com/bookgifts

The greater potential of living from wisdom

'Our separation from the natural world may have
given us the fruits of technology and science, but it has
left us bereft of any instinctual connection to the spiritual dimension of life.'[66] These are the words of Sufi
mystic and author Llewellyn Vaughan-Lee. He argues
that, as humans, we are often misled by our thinking
mind and the illusion of its separation from the natural world. We tend to see ourselves as detached from
the divine and from nature, and this he asserts lies at
the core of so much of our social and ecological crises.
This is because, as he continues, there is an undeni-
able 'connection between our soul and the soul of the
world, the knowing that we are all part of one living,
spiritual being.'[67]

I resonate with this and I believe strongly at this
point in my life and work that there is no such thing

as true inner strength without wisdom. There is an intelligence that runs through nature and all creation. Divorced from that intelligence, we tend to create suffering for ourselves and others, but connected to that intelligence, we find wholeness, inner peace and – our greatest source of strength as human beings – wisdom.

In our modern world, school systems, workplaces and the culture in general do not emphasise enough the importance of wisdom or awareness. As a rule, there is no training in cultivating these capacities, although this is slowly beginning to change. The focus is far more on intellectual intelligence than on wisdom. As Harvard biologist E O Wilson famously said, 'We are drowning in information, while starving for wisdom.'[68] Because of this deficiency of wisdom our modern world is an environment where it's easy to get lost in, and driven by, the thinking mind and its conditioned survival-based thinking patterns to the point of being chronically stressed, overwhelmed and dissatisfied or even burnt out, anxious or depressed.

When our living in the world is divorced from our deeper being, we often find ourselves pushed through life by the momentum of the modern world, never stopping long enough to take stock and ask the big questions. Are my actions aligned with my values? Am I fulfilled? Am I taking care of the things that truly matter to me – my body, my loved ones, the planet?

Without connection to our deep self and its wisdom, we can so easily fall into conditioned patterns of belief and behaviour that may not serve us, may not be making us happy nor healthy and may even be leading us, as a species, down paths that are highly unwise – threatening our very existence and the health of this planet we live on.

As David Attenborough observes, 'To continue to survive, humans require more than intelligence. We require wisdom.'[69] There has never been a more important time for us to reclaim our awareness and live from wisdom. If we can do that, not only do we gain a happier, healthier and more meaningful life for ourselves, but we also contribute to a world where we have greater capacity to live more sustainably, more deliberately and more peacefully. We can live with less anxiety, hate, greed and reactivity and with more care, compassion, wisdom, understanding and joy. We can live with more love and less fear.

Each time you practise inhabiting the present moment and connecting with your deeper self and its wisdom, know that you are not just benefiting yourself. Your inner strength will flow out from you and affect the people you know, everyone you meet and in some small way ripple out to touch the whole world. You become a locus of sanity, love and wisdom in this crazy world. So thank you for being here, for reading these words and for practising deep resilience. Deep bow and much gratitude to you.

Remember: all the benefits and transformation can only be achieved through *being* aware, *being* mindful. In other words, conceptual understanding is not enough when it comes to cultivating wisdom.

It's not enough to read about it, talk about it or watch talks about it. It needs to be practised and experienced first-hand for the positive changes to take place. Your capacity to access your deeper self through mindful awareness will grow more stable and accessible with every single practice, every mindful breath, every time you pause to catch yourself, every time you shift above the line.

Summary

In this second step of the RISE process, Inhabiting the Present Moment, we have taken a big leap forward. In Step 1, you prepared the way: you did the work to defuse from unhelpful thinking patterns, changed your relationship with thoughts and emotions, and learned how to redirect your mind in ways that uplift, empower and support you. You learned how to grow the good inside you and embrace life again. All of that has brought you to a point where you now have the tools to tap into your greatest sources of inner strength. You have learned to build a greater awareness and connect to your deep self. The more you practise the techniques and exercises in this chapter, the more you will find yourself able to live from wisdom and able to access your inherent strength. With every single practice, you are becoming more and more deeply resilient.

11

Step 3: Stay Connected To Your Values

Having worked through the first two steps of the Deep Resilience Method, you are now well equipped to recognise and regulate unhelpful mental and emotional thinking patterns such as rumination, worry, stress, negativity and self-doubt. You have also learned how to tap into the wisdom and power within you – that ability to find and inhabit the present moment. These are the first two steps in the RISE method; now we move on to the third step: Stay Connected to Your Values.

The practices in this book are fairly simple in and of themselves, but that doesn't mean they are always easy to do. It can be tricky to break free of FEAR, and we can find ourselves caught in its grip over and over again. Fortunately, the tools that you have learned in the Deep Resilience Method are powerful allies and will help you to shift out of these unhelpful patterns. But we can do so much more than simply live our lives trying not to get pushed around by stress, struggle and disempowerment. By staying connected to our values, we are *pulled* though challenges by a clear and solid sense of purpose.

In this chapter, you will see why understanding our core values is so important. You will identify your own core values and learn how to connect with them in a way that changes your whole orientation for navigating life in both good times and bad.

The power of purpose

Viktor Frankl had been a highly respected psychiatrist in Austria when, in 1944, he was transported to the infamous Auschwitz concentration camp. Frankl and his fellow prisoners had everything taken from them: their possessions, jobs, their families, friends, physical freedom – even their names (they were given numbers instead), their clothing and the hair on their bodies.

Most of their family members were murdered or died from starvation and ill treatment in the camps, including Frankl's wife, mother and brother, and for years they endured unfathomable horrors and suffering in the death camps, but there was one thing that remained truly their own: they could choose their attitude and response to any given thought, emotion or set of circumstances. This was a key realisation for Frankl and would be the catalyst for his future work.

Against all odds, Frankl survived and only a few months after his release, he wrote his most famous book, *Man's Search for Meaning*.[70] It chronicled his experience in the camps and introduced a new type of psychotherapy, logotherapy (from the Greek word *logos* and roughly translating as 'healing through meaning'). Logotherapy sought to explain how some human beings could be unbelievably resilient in impossible circumstances and argued that this is possible only when they remain connected to a deeper sense of purpose and meaning in life. Frankl asserted that human life is primarily a quest for meaning. This challenged Freud's theories that human beings are motivated only to seek pleasure and to avoid pain.

During his time in the concentration camps, Frankl observed that those around him who did not lose their sense of purpose and meaning were able to remain much more resilient and survived much longer than those who did not. They were able to find some peace and purpose to their existence and even to deepen their sense of spiritual life in the middle of it all:

> We who lived in concentration camps can
> remember the men who walked through the
> huts comforting others, giving away their
> last piece of bread. They may have been few
> in number, but they offer sufficient proof
> that everything can be taken from a man but
> one thing: the last of the human freedoms –
> to choose one's attitude in any given set of
> circumstances, to choose one's own way.[71]

Seeing the examples of how some endured, found meaning and spread kindness when others tipped into fear, hopelessness or gave up, Frankl began to focus on finding meaning in his own way by being helpful to others whenever he felt himself losing hope or felt helpless, frightened or alone and in this way he stayed connected to a meaningful vision for his future. When he was finally released, he continued to focus on being a force for good in the world, and, through his writings and teachings, looked to alleviate suffering and help others to find more meaning in their lives and inner strength.

Nelson Mandela spent twenty-seven years in prison after being arrested for fighting against apartheid and injustice. Despite having his freedom taken away, being separated from his loved ones and confined to a small prison cell, he too stayed focused on his greater meaning and purpose.

In his autobiography, *Long Walk to Freedom*, he described looking out the window of his cell and seeing those outside of different skin colours, recognising and reflecting on what he felt to be a fundamental truth:

> No one is born hating another person because
> of colour of his skin, or his background, or his
> religion. People must learn to hate, and if they
> can learn to hate, they can be taught to love,
> for love comes more naturally to the human
> heart than its opposite.[72]

During his long years in prison, Mandela felt enormous pain from the separation from his loved ones. He also had to receive the news of his daughter's death and grappled with serious illness. Through all of this, however, he refused to give up on his own values and never lost sight of his vision for a better future: 'Prison – far from breaking our spirits – made us more determined to continue with this battle until victory was won.'[73]

Mandela spent his time in prison gaining a law degree and corresponding with other prominent anti-apartheid activists. Even from inside a cell, he remained a powerful voice for change, and his steadfast commitment to his beliefs eventually led to his release in 1990. He then helped negotiate the end of apartheid in South Africa in a process that led to his election as its first democratically elected president and he was awarded a Nobel Peace Prize in 1993 for his efforts.

'I have cherished the ideal of a democratic and free society in which all persons live together in harmony and with equal opportunities,' Mandela said in the speech he gave during the trial that ended in his incarceration.[74] For him, this was a dream worth persisting with, struggling and fighting for, and his steadfastness not only helped him to survive and thrive but it inspired and forever changed the world.

Both Frankl and Mandela understood something important: they could not control all of their external circumstances, but they could control their response to them. Although at times they were afraid, overwhelmed and angry, they were not defined by those fears. They were able to stand firm on what they believed in and be pulled by a greater force inside them.

Fortunately, most of us will never experience challenges as extreme as those faced by Frankl and Mandela, but we can learn to apply the same principles they used to navigate through hardship in our own lives. Imagine if we had a simple way to shift our focus so that when we are overwhelmed, afraid and lacking hope, we could find indomitable inner strength by staying connected to our values and then be pulled through challenges by a rock-solid sense of purpose and empowerment.

Identifying your core values

Guided by values instead of governed by fear

To return to our metaphor from earlier in the book, our values, together with mindfulness, are like the foundations of a house. A house built on a solid foundation will be stable and steady even in the most turbulent storms and wildest winds, but a house built on a weak foundation will start to break down and fall apart when bad weather hits. Even in the good weather, this house will not be strong and may start to crack. You are that house, and just like the house, you will feel stable, strong and resilient through the ups and downs of life if you are built on the solid foundations of an unshakable connectedness to your values.

Connectedness with your values has been shown to greatly improve levels of fulfilment and satisfaction in life,[75] and reduce anxiety and depression.[76] It is also a key component in self-actualisation; that is, the ability to reach your full potential and become the person you want to be.[77] Together, these factors all increase overall resilience.

A beautiful quote often used to describe Frankl's philosophy is: 'Between the stimulus and response, there is a space. And in that space lies our freedom and power to choose our responses. In our response lies our growth and our freedom.'[78]

No matter what life throws at us, no matter how disappointing, painful and unjust, we always maintain the power to choose who we will be in response to it, and how we will think, act and treat others and ourselves. This is a power that nothing and no one can take away and that we carry with us wherever we go.

As we touched on in Chapter 1, most people lack clarity when it comes to their values. They may know what they want to get away from – stress, low mood, anxiety, depression – but they can't articulate what they want to move towards. They have not yet identified their own core values and this creates a shaky foundation, which can more easily buckle under pressure. Clearly identifying your core values is critical to finding resilience in challenging times. Your values are your guiding light in the dark forest of life's challenges, lighting the way towards who you really are and what matters most to you, deep in your heart.

We all have values – they are as much a part of us as our blood type or our DNA and they are as unique to us as our individual thumbprints. Our core values determine what's genuinely important and meaningful to us.

Your values are:

- Your deepest desires for how you want to behave as a human being

- How you want to act on an ongoing basis

- Expressions of who you are and what matters to you most

- Your internal guiding principles for how you want to treat yourself, others and the world around you

- An internal compass that points to your own 'true North'

Examples of values are things like kindness, integrity, loyalty, courage, fun, fairness, spirituality, wellbeing, peacefulness, love, adventure, generosity, sustainability, justice, patience, persistence, creativity and mindfulness. There are hundreds of different values and we all have our own unique set of core values.

Your values are not:

- Goals that you reach an endpoint with

- Who you think you should be in order to fit in

- What anyone else thinks you should value

Values are not something we invent or conjure up; they are already there within us. We just need to unearth them and see and know them more clearly.

When the way you act is in alignment with your values, you're in your strength. Life may not always be easy, smooth or pleasant, but you'll be connected to a sense of empowerment, agency, meaning and purpose no matter what is happening in your circumstances. In contrast, when your actions don't align with your values, it's easy to feel disempowered, overwhelmed, discontented, disconnected from meaning and agency and unfulfilled. Without that strong foundation of connectedness with values, you'll tend to tip towards FEAR, struggle and stress. This is why making a conscious effort to identify your values and act in alignment with them is so critical to becoming deeply resilient.

A good go-to for gauging if the actions you are about to take are aligned with your core values is to check in with what your gut feelings or your heart are telling you. Listening to these deep feelings allows you to be more in tune with your needs, your wisdom and your heart's deepest desires.

It's important to note that there are no such things as 'right values' or 'wrong values'. It's a bit like taste in music: if I prefer classical music and you like pop, that doesn't mean that your taste is wrong and mine is right; it just means we have different tastes in music.

Similarly, we may hold different values from each other. Core values may also change over the course of our lifetime.

Values as expressions of our deeper nature

I think of values as our own unique expression of the wisdom of our deep nature, a particular individual expression of the seven strengths we learned about in Chapter 10 (love, clarity, peace, playful curiosity, courage, fulfilment and connection). The essence of our deepest nature is the same in all of us, but we each express it in our unique way.

We can think about our deep self as being like a diamond with many facets. The facets are all of our values, all of the different ways we express that deeper nature. But the core of the diamond is really the same in each of us, and is what Buddhists refer to as our Buddha nature.

When your mind is in survival mode, its main mission is to keep you safe from harm at whatever cost. It may therefore tip into conditioned patterns like overthinking, negativity, hostility and self-doubt in an innocent but misguided attempt to keep you alive. These thinking patterns can end up pushing you around, overwhelming you with stress, negativity and fear. By contrast, your values emanate from a deeper place within you. They keep you in touch with your authenticity, integrity, wisdom and what truly matters to you. Acting from your values gives you a sense of steadiness, purpose, certainty and strength within the storms of life. It pulls you towards the things that give you meaning, purpose, satisfaction and strength.

It is these sources of strength that you want to build awareness of, focus on and be guided by in your actions, as best you can. This is not about being reckless, overly idealistic or frivolous in our actions – we want to be effective, realistic and skilful – but about remaining steadfast in our connection to who we are and what matters to us the most. This focus on purpose serves as a pivot, enabling us to shift out of FEAR and into a place of deeper resilience.

Over the years, I have repeatedly used the following exercises with my clients to help them become clear on their values and grow a stronger and deeper connection with them. As you go through these exercises now to determine your own core values, see if you can be guided more by your gut feelings than by concern about what you should or shouldn't be valuing or what other people will think. Try not to overthink it in general – it's often best to go with your first instinct.

EXERCISE 16: Ten-minute practice: Discover your core values

Look thought the list of values in the table below.

Acceptance	Altruism	Boldness
Accomplishment	Ambition	Bravery
Adaptability	Balance	Brilliance
Adventure	Beauty	Calmness

Care	Empowerment	Health
Challenge	Enjoyment	Honesty
Commitment	Enthusiasm	Honor
Community	Equality	Hope
Compassion	Excellence	Humility
Confidence	Exploration	Humour
Connection	Expression	Imagination
Consistency	Fairness	Individuality
Contentment	Faith	Innovation
Contribution	Family	Integrity
Courage	Foresight	Intelligence
Courtesy	Fortitude	Joy
Creativity	Freedom	Justice
Curiosity	Friendliness	Kindness
Daring	Friendship	Leadership
Dedication	Fulfilment	Learning
Dependability	Fun	Love
Dignity	Generosity	Loyalty
Discipline	Giving	Mastery
Discovery	Grit	Mindfulness
Diversity	Growth	Moderation
Efficiency	Happiness	Nature
Empathy	Harmony	Openness

Optimism	Reverence	Tolerance
Order	Sensuality	Tradition
Passion	Serenity	Tranquillity
Patience	Service	Transparency
Peace	Sharing	Trustworthiness
Persistence	Simplicity	Truth
Playfulness	Spirituality	Understanding
Presence	Spontaneity	Uniqueness
Productivity	Stewardship	Unity
Prosperity	Structure	Vitality
Quality	Surprise	Wellbeing
Respect	Sustainability	Wisdom
Responsibility	Thoughtfulness	Wonder

As you look through the list, you may find that you relate to all of the values in some way shape or form but some will stand out as being more important to you. Write out the values in a notebook or on a piece of paper, and place a score beside each value, choosing whether it is not very important to you (1), important to you (2), or very important to you (3).

This list of values is not exhaustive, and you may have other words to describe your own values, so feel free to write in any extra values that come to mind while you're going through the activity.

The next step is to note your top twelve values according to the scores you've given above. This is your shortlist of the most important and meaningful qualities with which to align your way of being.

Now see if you can refine your list even further, down to five to seven core values. What are the values that matter to you most?

While you may relate to many values in some ways, these core values represent something of your personal 'true North'. When you are living in alignment with these values, you will always find a place of solidity and strength within yourself and clarity to guide you through.

A wise teacher once said to me that the essence of awakening to our full potential as humans is just a short journey. 'About this far,' he said, indicating the distance between his head and his heart. 'All we need to do is make the journey from here (pointing to his head) to here (pointing to his heart).' In other words, by letting go of being pushed around by our survival-based thinking patterns and dropping into a focus on presence and purpose, we can awaken to our deeper sources of strength and our highest potentials as human beings.

EXERCISE 17: Two-minute exercise: Tune in to the strength in your heart

Remember, presence and purpose (Inhabit the Present Moment and Stay Connected to Your Values) are ways of connecting with our own deepest being, our true nature. This is a power far greater than doubt, insecurity, greed, shame or stress.

So when you need to find strength, become present, get still, listen to your heart and trust that strength is within you. Don't let the noise and fear in your mind drown out the silent strength in your heart. Remember:

- You are strong.
- You have a deep resilience within you that is far greater than fear.
- You have all the strength and wisdom you need, accessible to you at any moment.

One of the simplest and fastest ways I know to tap into that reservoir of strength and wisdom inside is this practice. Let's try it now so you can see how it feels:

- Place a hand or both hands over the centre of your chest.
- Shift your attention out of your head and bring your focus to the centre of your chest.
- Take a few slightly deeper slower breaths with your attention there, becoming more and more fully present. Do this for around a minute (or longer if you care to).
- When you are ready, ask yourself, *What is my highest intention in this moment?*

If you ever feel lost, confused, overwhelmed, frightened, angry or in turmoil, come back to this simple practice and let it connect you back to your heart, back to presence and purpose, your greatest inner strengths.

You can access a guided audio version of this meditation (as well as all the other meditations and some additional resources) at www.melliobrien.com/bookgifts

Now that you have uncovered your core values and learned how to stay connected to them, you are better able to not let yourself be pushed around by unhelpful thoughts and reactive patterns. With this new clarity on your values and what matters to you, you can act with greater intention and move forward with your life with more confidence and agency.

This is the roadmap to deep resilience: anchoring yourself in purpose and presence, letting the deep self take the lead and living from awareness and wisdom. In this way, you will always be more powerful than fear.

Summary

Building on the momentum of the first two steps, we are now on the home stretch of your journey through the Deep Resilience Method. Earlier, you laid the groundwork by developing the skills of mental strength and emotional strength; in this chapter you have completed the third step of deep resilience and now have solidified your ability to tap into your wisdom, your spiritual strength.

When you apply these tools, you'll be able to become a more integrated, wise, authentic and effective person and enjoy your life more fully.

This has been a practical and exercise-based chapter. You homed in on your core values and learned techniques to connect with them so they can guide the way. You now know how and when to tap into them when you need to find your strength.

From your journey through this book so far, you have now accumulated a suite of techniques and tools to help you stay mentally, emotionally and also spiritually strong, allowing you to become a more integrated, empowered, resilient and wise person.

In the next and final step, Engage in Empowered Action, you will learn how to take everything you've learned so far and integrate it into your daily life. You will make an Empowered Action Plan to give you clarity on how to make your daily life more in alignment with your values. This will mean that you can immediately apply that greater strength in real and concrete ways to whatever you are going through, now and in the future.

12

Step 4: Engage In Empowered Action

To become deeply resilient, we must consistently take empowered action. This means acting with awareness and in ways that align with our core values. So far, we've built your capacity to Recognise and Regulate Thoughts and Emotions in healthy and skilful ways, we've seen how to access the wisdom of your core self by Inhabiting the Present Moment, and we've also learned how to Stay Connected to Your Values. Through these steps, you have built mental emotional and spiritual strength.

In this, the final step of the Deep Resilience Method, we will take everything you've learned and integrate it into your daily life and your way of being.

The hero's journey

You might not think you have much in common with Harry Potter, Wonder Woman, Luke Skywalker or the heroes from your favourite fairytales but, according to Carl Jung, Joseph Campbell and others, we all do. They assert that the main characters in our stories, movies and myths offer us universal archetypes representing a kind of map or blueprint for self-realisation; that is, making the self *real* (by connecting to and acting out of who we really are in our deepest nature).

The hero's journey is a storytelling structure that was identified and outlined by the mythologist Joseph Campbell in his 1949 classic book, *The Hero with a Thousand Faces*.[79] In it, he unpacks the idea, first developed by psychologist Carl Jung,[80] that all humans share certain universal but unconscious mental models for how to navigate the ups and downs of life, awaken their potential and become 'fully developed' or self-realised human beings.

According to Campbell, these internal mental models have been consistently and universally expressed through the stories we've told ourselves and each other, from ancient myths and legends to the latest Hollywood blockbusters. He argued that within all of these stories is embedded an archetypal story, a 'monomyth' that he named 'the hero's journey'. By retelling some variation on the main elements of this story, people throughout time and across all cultures have passed down key life lessons.

At its core, the hero's journey is one of inner transformation, typically featuring a few key milestones. To fully realise and express their true self, the hero must voyage out from what is familiar, certain and safe; face and overcome their demons, temptations and fears; and stay true to their values. The story also stars archetypal characters such as villains, cowards, helpful guides and brave companions that reflect elements of our psyche and the archetypal patterns that lead us towards or away from wisdom, fulfilment and love.

The hero's story therefore offers us both warnings against being led astray in life and instructions on how to unlock the best within us and realise our full potential by following the arc of the hero's journey. Through their journey, the hero learns to rise above being led and dominated by ego and fear, and unfurls to become their truest self. This process of self-realisation and self-actualisation is the essence of the quest. We do not need to venture out alone: 'for the heroes of all time have gone before us; the labyrinth is thoroughly known; we have only to follow the thread of the hero-path.'[81] We learn from the stories of the heroes how to realise our potential and best live our lives.

One of the lessons central to the monomyth is that it is a very bad idea to try to ignore or run away from the things you fear the most or find hard to face. So too is getting fused with our ego in the form of unhelpful thoughts that fuel greed and hatred, insecurity and delusion, or living your life unaligned with values and wisdom.

The villain and/or the coward in all the stories usually ends up the same way: time and time again we see how those who get fused with unhelpful thoughts and fears (in other words, overtaken by their ego) and lose touch with their values end up turning away from the 'hero-path' and towards the dark side. Filled with fear, insecurity, greed or hatred, they pursue an unwise course (ignoring the cost to others and to themselves) that ultimately ends up leading to their downfall.

According to the monomyth, when we take delight in watching the cowards and/or villains finally face their comeuppance, this reflects our desire to kill our own greed, fear and ignorance and connect to the authenticity and strength of our deepest self. A satisfactory completion of the hero's mission involves bravely facing up to who or what they fear most, staying unwaveringly true to their values, and returning to their normal world but totally transformed, now able to live in the ordinary world as a hero.

Sadly, we usually find out in the end that the villain was once an ordinary person 'just like us' who didn't know how to deal with their pain and lost their way, getting stuck in ever deepening cycles of FEAR. In the really good stories, the villain has just enough humanity or vulnerability to make them relatable, helping us to understand better what led them to become who they were. The coward is an everyday person, not quite as lost as the villain, but who lives disconnected from presence and purpose. Theirs is a shallow life. They too are often party to their own demise and this archetype too serves as a warning to all who hear it.

Odysseus, Persephone, Shakespeare's Henry V, Harry Potter, Moana, Luke Skywalker, Black Panther and Spider-Man: all are fictional characters who have made the hero's journey. Even though they were not perfect, made mistakes, had flaws and felt fear, ultimately, they were able to face their biggest fears and darkest demons and, by staying connected with their deeper nature, they rose triumphant.

Wholehearted living

The story of the hero reminds us of a timeless truth: by facing our fears and demons and bringing awareness to them, we strip them of their power. By staying connected with our deepest sources of strength and acting with wisdom and awareness, even when it's hard to do, fear and egoic patterns can no longer define or defeat us. The hero in each of us is born in every moment we connect with, and act from, the deep strength within us.

The hero's journey is a map outlining how to achieve a wholehearted, meaningful and fulfilling life. It begins with defusing from unhelpful mental/ emotional/behavioural patterns and culminates in embodying and acting from purpose and presence. Decades of psychological research has shown that our life satisfaction, our ability to stay resilient in the face of inevitable fear, stress and sad experiences depends, not so much on how many difficult things we experience or even on their intensity, but on the way we deal with them. Approaching the ups and downs of our human journey from a place of deep resilience is key to a wholehearted life.

Unlike in the movies, deep resilience rarely takes the form of grandiose or heroic acts – it's usually much simpler. It may be a quiet choice to do what is right over what is convenient; standing up for something you believe in; being patient when someone pushes your buttons; taking small but significant steps towards meaningful goals even when they push you out of your comfort zone; looking personal insecurities, fears and inner demons in the eye and meeting them with understanding and wisdom, saying, *OK, you're here. I see you. You're allowed to be here. I can work with you.* It might be the decision to be kind to a stranger or to look after your own needs even as you look after others as best you can.

It's also about seeing that who you are is big enough to contain all of your feelings, urges, impulses and even all of your fears, and is able to accept these parts of you, without being crushed or controlled by them. By connecting with and acting from what is deepest and truest in you, your inner demons won't defeat or define you; in fact, you can meet them with wisdom, steadiness and kindness, end the war within and make peace with them.

Think of deep resilience less as a destination and more as a moment-by-moment choice we can make. In any moment we can choose strength. We can act from strength. That choice is always available no matter where we find ourselves.

As we go about life, there will often be times when we find ourselves suddenly faced with one of our inner demons or trying to navigate through our own dark and shadowy places. Sometimes it comes in the form of a formidable adversary – an old wound that triggers our deepest fears and strongest reactivity; other times it might be just a little niggling thought pattern causing us a bit of background stress, annoyance or discomfort. Our challenges and trials may include dealing with regrets about the past, anxiety and worry about the future, insecurity about ourselves, cravings, doubts or sadness. Whatever they may be, they will often try to lure you into FEAR, pull you below the line and lead you away from strength. Each of these moments is a choice point. You can choose deep resilience again and again. It will always be there for you.

The Deep Resilience Method will guide you through the steps of the hero's journey in those moments and help you unlock and harness your inner strength, awareness and wisdom, even in the darkest moments of your life.

In this last part of the process, Engage in Empowered Action, we will pull together everything we've learned so far and take the final steps on this adventure together.

What is empowered action?

Empowered action means acting with awareness (presence) and in alignment with our values (purpose). In order to do this, one of the most important principles to remember is to always stay focused on your zone of control, then act.

Your zone of control

In a crisis, challenge or a difficult time of any sort, a certain amount of stress, anxiety and upset are normal and natural responses. However we often ramp this up by getting caught up in overthinking and fixating about all sorts of things that are totally out of our control, or that we have very little influence over: what other people are doing or not doing; how we think things should be; how world events like economic crises or financial crashes, pandemics, natural disasters or wars will unfold or how governments are handling things; what is going to happen in the future.

It's natural for the human mind to fixate on all of these things, but it's not helpful. In fact, the research indicates that the more we focus on things outside of our control, the more helpless, overwhelmed and anxious we're likely to feel.[82]

As such, an important thing to do to find deep resilience and empowerment in hard times is to focus on what *is* in your control, let go of (defuse from) what *isn't* and then take empowered action where you can.

Stoic philosopher Epictetus asserted the importance of this principle when he wrote:

Happiness and freedom begin with a clear understanding of one principle: Some things are within our control, and some things are not. The chief task in life is simply this: to identify and separate matters so that I can say clearly to myself which are externals not under my control, and which have to do with the choices I actually control.

To stay focused on our zone of control, we need to make a clear distinction between what's within and what's outside of it. For example, you can't control what happens in the future. You cannot change what happened in the past. You can't control other people. And you cannot control all of your thoughts and feelings.

Within our control are our own attitudes and our actions. This includes things like what we focus on; the meanings we make; how we treat others; goals we set; how we spend our time; what environments we put ourselves in; what media, books and information we consume; how productive we are; the support we gather for ourselves; whether that's therapy, coaching or courses we take; what we eat; our sleep routine; who we spend time with, and so on.

In the diagram below are two circles. The outer circle contains various things we cannot control – wars erupting around the world, the state of the economy, other people's actions, whether people like you or not, the problems in society, political systems, the way other people drive, the weather, climate change, how others treat you and so on – and the inner circle contains things that we can.

A lot of us get stuck in fear and struggle because we focus on things that are outside of our control. Especially common is a fixation on what other people say and do; how others perceive us; what will be the outcome of our actions and what will happen in the future; what happened in the past that we wish was different or we feel should not have happened; whether or not life gives us what we want; painful events in life such as heartbreak, loss, or the inevitability of ageing, illness and impermanence. The more we focus on what is outside of our zone of control, the more frantic, disempowered, distressed, frustrated, disappointed or angry we will feel. And the more likely it is we will become reactive and stuck in FEAR.

In contrast, the more we focus on what is inside our zone of control, the more empowered, effective and influential we become. While our zone of control is smaller than that which is outside of it, it's where our power lies. If we look deeply, we can see that most of the time, events themselves are not the root cause of our suffering and stress, but rather it is our resistance to (including our desire to change) that which we have little or no control over.

Learning to accept what we cannot control and consistently focus on what is within your control enables you to stay deeply resilient. This will enable you to move towards positive changes, take effective and skilful actions and act on your values and be the person you want to be in the middle of it all.

EXERCISE 18: Two-minute exercise: Find your zone of control

Whenever you find yourself stuck in overthinking or fixating on things outside of your control, try these three steps.

First, centre yourself with a few mindful breaths. Become present.

Then, ask yourself (and answer, on paper or out loud):

- What is my concern?
- What is within my control?

- What matters most to me (tune in to your values) and what helpful actions can I take that align with them, no matter how small?

Finally, make an intention to practise acceptance of what's out of your control.

If you find it helpful, mentally say a mantra of acceptance, like, *The rest is as it is*, or *The rest will be as it will be.*

You can access a guided audio version of this meditation (as well as all the other meditations in this book and some additional resources) at www.melliobrien.com/bookgifts

---

Remember, trying to influence or change what is not in your zone of control will only drain your energy, cause you suffering and make you reactive. When you can't control what's happening, focus on controlling the way you are *responding* to what's happening. That is where the power is.

Your Empowered Action Plan

We spent some time in the previous chapter identifying our values and learning to connect with them. While knowing our values is crucial, keep in mind that they are just ideas if you don't act on them. Without expressing them through your actions they are not very useful or helpful at all. Once you have identified your values, you need to actually engage in action guided by them. This means committing to things you can do that are in line with those values.

In this section, we will be exploring how aligned you are currently with your values in different domains of your life, and then identifying some values-based goals that will bring you closer to your own true North. This Empowered Action Plan is something you can take with you into daily life, to check in with regularly and use as an ongoing guide to keep bolstering your inner strength.

Before we get started, let's first revisit the difference between goals and values:

- **Values** are inner qualities. They are about who we want to be and how we want to live our lives. They are like a compass that keeps us headed in our desired direction. Values are something we aim to embody on an ongoing basis.

- **Goals** are distinctly different. They are the specific ways you intend to execute your values. They are things you can tick off the to-do list. Goals are something you can achieve at a specific point in time.

Being courteous is a value; turning up on time to the party is a goal. Being generous is a value; giving 10% of your income each year to charity is a goal. Spirituality is a value; meditating each day for thirty minutes is a goal.

By identifying goals that express your values, you'll find a sense of steadiness, strength and confidence inside yourself that you can rely on even when life is hard and uncertain.

EXERCISE 19: Fifteen-minute exercise: Towards true North

This exercise helps you identify, and move towards, your own 'true North'.

Step 1: Take a moment to look back at your list of core values drawn up in Exercise 16.

Step 2: Below, five domains are listed: work, people, health, growth and play. Take a moment to understand what each domain includes.

Take a moment to understand what each domain covers:

Work refers to your workplace (including unpaid and voluntary work), career and education. Think about how you want to treat your clients, customers and colleagues. What personal attributes do you want to bring to your work?

People refers to relationships, intimacy, closeness, friendship and those you bond with in your life. It includes relationships with your partner, family, friends, coworkers, community members and others. What sort of relationships do you want to build? How do you want to be in these relationships? What personal qualities do you want to express and how do you aspire to show up?

Health refers to how you take care of your own physical and mental wellbeing. This may include self-care, health checks, getting out into nature, exercise, good nutrition, meditation, therapy and addressing health risk factors like smoking.

Growth refers to your ongoing development as a human being as well as your sense of spirituality. This may include organised religion, individual expressions of spirituality, personal development, developing life skills or anything that helps you grow and develop as a person.

Play is about your leisure time: how you play, relax, stimulate or enjoy yourself; your hobbies or other activities for rest, recreation, fun and creativity.

Now that you are familiar with each domain, on a piece of paper, write down the values that are most important to you for each of these domains of life. The values may be the same as your core values, or you might find that different domains of life call forth additional values for you.

Step 3: On a piece of paper, write down a score of 1–5 to represent where you stand today in regard to how aligned you are with your values in each of these domains. A 1 means not very aligned; a 3 means you're doing OK but there is room for improvement; and 5 is 'true North', meaning that you are living closely aligned with your values in that area of life.

Step 4: Look at your answers. For any areas that have not scored 5, think about some actions you can take that would help increase your score and move you into closer alignment with your values. These actions could be small steps towards a particular meaningful goal or daily actions and habits that reflect who you want to be as a person. Try to identify and note down at least three but up to six empowered actions (across all domains) you are willing to take within the next month to move closer to your true North. Give these a heading of 'My empowered action goals for the next 30 days'.

Once you complete this exercise, you should have at least three empowered actions written down that you are committing to undertaking in your daily life in the next 30 days. To make this more concrete, you can choose to set a completion date and put this in your calendar.

This exercise is one that you can use on an ongoing basis to help you stay on track, in alignment with your values and in your power. You might like to set a reminder to check in monthly, quarterly or even a handful of times a year and keep adjusting your course as necessary to ensure you are continually maintaining and growing deep resilience.

Keep your eye on the prize

As with so many of the important things in life, we must accept that empowered action comes with trade-offs and can have unwanted consequences such as unpleasant thoughts, feelings or results.

For example, if we follow our value of justice and stand up for someone who has been treated unfairly at work, we may experience unwanted thoughts like: *I don't know if I can really do this, What if it doesn't work?* or *What impacts will this have on me?* We may also find that uncomfortable feelings and emotions come up in response to living our values, such as anxiety before giving a presentation, before asking someone on a date or when setting off on a trip.

Throughout the writing of this book, I have had thoughts of self-doubt visit me: *What if people don't like this book? What if it gets bad reviews? Why didn't I just get a safer and easier job?!* Even though these thoughts are a bit unpleasant, I am willing to experience them because I know that they are a natural part of me moving towards my goal of sharing these words with you.

Accepting the trade-offs doesn't necessarily imply that we welcome these side effects of moving towards our true North – we are not likely to enjoy them – but it does mean that we are willing to experience and allow those feelings and thoughts as an unavoidable and natural part of living in alignment with wisdom and in accordance with our values.

We will also need resolve to walk the path of true North. There will be times when our imperfections, weaknesses and flaws show up; moments of failure or setback and times when we lose touch with our values and veer off course. All of that is normal. Every time we find ourselves off course, we can simply begin again. But stumbling, falling and trying again should be considered normal parts of the journey. We will need to have persistence when we confront the inevitable obstacles and hurdles that we will meet when taking empowered action. The path to living our values will not be perfect or easy, but it's worth taking.

The key is to keep your eye on the prize. Keep a strong connection to what matters to you most. Keep reminding yourself of your values and the vision you have for yourself and your life. Keep connecting with the wisdom inside you. Each time you do this, you galvanise and grow your inner strength.

Bringing it all together

Now that we have covered all four steps in the RISE framework, we're going to bring it all together in an on-the-go micro practice that you can use in any difficult moment to stay deeply resilient.

As we discussed way back in Chapter 1, the RISE framework can be used as both a macro practice and a micro practice. As a macro practice, the skills the method builds can be applied and used as an overall philosophy and approach for how to be deeply resilient in your life; as a micro practice, it is a four-step process you can utilise in any given moment when you want to tap into your inner strength.

Any time that you find yourself below the mental strength line or struggling with states of stress, fear or suffering, walk through these four steps to quickly and easily shift out of FEAR and instead RISE.

Remember, FEAR is characterised by four key elements. It's when we're:

- Fused with thoughts
- Engaged in a struggle with emotions
- Acting in ways that are life draining or out of alignment with our values
- Remote from the present moment – and our deeper nature

The antidote to this is to RISE.

Here's how you can use this micro practice to connect to your inner strength in any given moment. It can be done in as little as thirty seconds once you're familiar with it, and you will always have it with you wherever you go.

EXERCISE 20: Two-minute exercise: The RISE micro practice, an on-the-go antidote to FEAR

Try bringing to mind a stressful situation you experienced recently.

Now work your way through the RISE micro practice by following the four steps:

Step 1: Recognise and Regulate Thoughts and Emotions: Use any of the defusion tools you've learned in this book to unhook from unhelpful mental and emotional patterns. (For example, try the Name It and Tame It steps from Chapter 5.) Mentally say to yourself (with a kindly and friendly tone) *Thanks, Mind! But that's not very helpful.* Then focus on the feeling of your breath and take three deep breaths.

Step 2: Inhabit the Present Moment: Shift your attention deeply into this present moment and engage with your senses. Connect with the stillness and strength inside you.

Step 3: Stay Connected to Your Values: Remind yourself of your values in some way. You might like to place a hand on your heart and/or ask yourself, *What is my highest intention in this moment?*

Step 4: Engage in Empowered Action: Let your next actions (if action is needed) be guided by awareness and purpose.

With these four simple steps, you can RISE from FEAR and quickly connect with deep resilience in any situation or circumstance.

Summary

This final step brings you to the culmination of the RISE framework. Everything you have learned and worked through in the last twelve chapters has equipped you with all the tools you need to practise deep resilience in your life. You now also have a plan for how to take empowered action that will be a source of strength and positive momentum in the days to come, kicking off a virtuous upwards spiral that will help you self-actualise, flourish and become a force for greater good in the world.

Conclusion

Congratulations on embracing the Deep Resilience Method and for taking this time to invest in yourself and in your own healing, transformation and growth. I have deep respect and gratitude for you for being a person who is walking the path of inner strength and, by default, being a part of the movement towards a more peaceful, sustainable and equal world.

Now that you know the Deep Resilience Method, you have equipped yourself with a powerful and practical toolkit that you will have with you for the rest of your life. The strategies you've learned in these pages can be applied in your personal life, your professional life, your love life and even your spiritual life.

You can use this book as a companion. You can always go back through the chapters of this book and use it as a resource for life.

I encourage you to maintain self-awareness around your FEAR-based patterns. When FEAR arises, Recognise and Regulate, Inhabit the Present Moment, Stay Connected to Your Values and Engage in Empowered Action. Practise these skills over and over again and they will eventually become second nature.

The situations you will face going forwards will not always be within your control, but you will always have the power to choose your response. You can always RISE to what is happening.

Nothing can take that power away from you, no matter what you are facing.

So keep RISEing, friend. Keep practising deep resilience.

Remember: keep your eye on the prize.

Keep defusing from fear-based patterns and let your deeper self take the lead. Keep choosing strength. Keep choosing life. Keep choosing love, over and over again. No matter how many times you stumble or falter, simply RISE and begin again.

Remember that to be human is to experience difficult emotions and thoughts, to experience vulnerability and difficulty and to be a bit messy sometimes. That's not wrong or bad. It's just part of being human.

Your mind is not your enemy; it is your ally. However, it needs you to lead and guide it, because it will tend to tip into FEAR when things get tough. It is always trying to keep you safe, but living from

Deep Resilience better equips you to navigate our modern world.

Remember, although our world is beautiful and precious, it is also troubled, so keep your wits about you. Trust your own wisdom and inner compass as the ultimate authority on what's right for you. It will keep you moving towards your true North. Don't be afraid to challenge the status quo and find your own authentic path forward.

You now know how to tap into your wisdom, purpose and strength and can embrace the life that you truly want to live, instead of the way that the fear-based patterns in the mind or society tell you to live.

You are strong.

You have an unshakable core of love, courage, goodness and other admirable qualities and values. You are whole. And you already belong. You belong to life and you are never alone. You are much stronger, greater, wiser and more resilient than your mind can ever grasp.

Even in the midst of challenges, stresses and struggles, you always have access to this knowing, in the deepest part of yourself, to your deepest resilience. You can never lose it. It's with you wherever you go, no matter how dark the path.

Take your focus there now. To that stillness and aliveness inside you.

What does it want you to know?

Who does it want you to be?

What changes does it want you to make?

What actions does it want you to take?

How does it want you to serve and make a difference?

Keep listening to that wisdom within. Don't let the noise in your mind drown out the strength in your heart.

Remember, this was never about changing yourself. It's about *knowing* yourself deeply and *being* yourself fully.

Because who you are is a being full of love, wisdom and strength.

You've got this.

All the strength, wisdom and love you need to RISE is right here and now. It always will be.

I believe in you. And I'm walking the path beside you.

Thank you for your practice, for walking this path to a stronger world with me. My gratitude is with you. My heart is with you. I wish you all the best on your own adventure through this one wild, precious and crazy life.

Melli.

Next Steps

There are several resources available to support your continued journey to becoming deeply resilient:

- **Get the bonus guided coaching audios and meditations:** If you haven't already, you can unlock exclusive downloadable guided meditations and coaching audios to help you implement and integrate the key concepts from this book. Unlock your gifts at www.melliobrien. com/bookgifts

- **Join the community for ongoing support:** To get ongoing free tips and teachings on the Deep Resilience Method and to stay informed about upcoming events (including regular free live

events), sign up for the newsletter at www.
melliobrien.com

- **Tune in and subscribe to the *Deep Resilience*
  podcast for free weekly teachings:** Find it
  wherever you listen to your podcasts

- **Start the thirty-day course:** The Deep Resilience
  Experience is a deeply transformative thirty-day
  journey to unshakable inner strength. As you
  master the Deep Resilience Method you'll find
  fast relief from stress and suffering, tap back into
  your greatest strengths and create rapid positive
  change in your life. Emerge feeling stronger,
  wiser and more peaceful than you've ever been
  before and armed with powerful new tools and
  insights that will last a lifetime. Find out more at
  www.melliobrien.com/30daycourse

Notes

1 World Health Organization, *World Mental Health Report: Transforming mental health for all* (WHO, 2022), https://iris.who.int/bitstream/handle/10665/356119/9789240049338-eng.pdf?sequence=1&isAllowed=y, accessed 12 May 2024

2 American Psychological Association, 'More than a quarter of U.S. adults say they're so stressed they can't function' (APA, 19 October 2022), www.apa.org/news/press/releases/2022/10/multiple-stressors-no-function, accessed 10 May 2024

3 R Berman, 'Eco-anxiety: 75% of young people say "the future is frightening"', *Medical News Today* (28 September 2021), www.medicalnewstoday.com/articles/eco-anxiety-75-of-young-people-say-the-future-is-frightening, accessed 12 May 2024

4 MJ Friedrich, 'Depression is the leading cause of disability around the world', *Journal of the American Medical Association*, 317/15 (2017), https://doi.org/10.1001/jama.2017.3826

5 G Mate, *The Myth of Normal: Illness, health and healing in a toxic culture* (Vermilion, 2022)

6   T Kasser, *The High Price of Materialism* (MIT Press, 2003)

7   L Winerman, 'Suppressing the "white bears"', *Monitor on Psychology*, 42/9 (2011), www.apa.org/monitor/2011/10/unwanted-thoughts, accessed 21 November 2024; DM Wegner and S Zanakos, 'Chronic thought suppression', *Journal of Personality*, 62/4 (1994), https://dtg.sites.fas.harvard.edu/DANWEGNER/pub/Wegner&Zanakos1994.pdf, accessed 21 November 2024

8   M Cullen, 'How to regulate your emotions without suppressing them', *Greater Good Magazine* (30 January 2020), https://greatergood.berkeley.edu/article/item/how_to_regulate_your_emotions_without_suppressing_them, accessed 23 May 2024

9   American Psychiatric Association, 'What is somatic symptom disorder?' (APA, August 2021), www.psychiatry.org/patients-families/somatic-symptom-disorder/what-is-somatic-symptom-disorder, accessed 13 May 2024

10 A broad overview of some of this research is provided by CE Ackerman, 'Life satisfaction theory and 4 contributing factors (+ scale)', *Positive Psychology* (6 November 2018), https://positivepsychology.com/life-satisfaction, accessed 14 May 2024

11 Research suggests that this has been true for at least 90% of human history: RB Lee and R Daly, 'Introduction: Foragers and others', in: *The Cambridge Encyclopedia of Hunters and Gatherers* (Cambridge University Press, 1999), pp1–20

12 The negativity bias has been extensively studied by the neuroscientist and psychologist John Cacioppo, among others.

13 S David, 'The gift and power of emotional courage' (TEDWomen, 2017), www.ted.com/talks/susan_david_the_gift_and_power_of_emotional_courage, accessed 15 May 2024

14 R Hanson and F Hanson, 'How to hardwire resilience into your brain', *Greater Good Magazine* (27 March 2018), https://greatergood.berkeley.edu/article/item/how_to_hardwire_resilience_into_your_brain, accessed 19 September 2024; ACM Garcia et al, 'Mindful self-care, self-compassion, and resilience among palliative care providers during the COVID-19 pandemic', *Journal of Pain Symptom*

Management, 64/1 (2022), pp49–57, www.jpsmjournal.com/article/S0885-3924(22)00469-9/fulltext

15 B Brown, *Braving the Wilderness: The quest for true belonging and the courage to stand alone* (Random House, 2017)

16 F Dostoyevsky, 'Winter notes on summer impressions', *Vremya* (February 1863)

17 DM Wegner et al, 'Paradoxical effects of thought suppression', *Journal of Personality and Social Psychology*, 53/1 (1987), pp5–13, https://doi.org/10.1037/0022-3514.53.1.5

18 K Neff, *Self-Compassion: The proven power of being kind to yourself* (William Morrow Paperbacks, 2018)

19 JG Breines and S Chen, 'Self-compassion increases self-improvement motivation', *Personality and Social Psychology Bulletin*, 38/9 (2012), pp1133–1143, https://pubmed.ncbi.nlm.nih.gov/22645164, accessed 15 January 2025

20 S Chen, 'Give yourself a break: The power of self-compassion', *Harvard Business Review* (September–October 2018), https://hbr.org/2018/09/give-yourself-a-break-the-power-of-self-compassion, accessed 15 January 2025; K Pace, 'Research shows that practicing self-compassion increases motivation', *Michigan State University Extension* (28 October 2016), accessed 15 January 2025

21 G Dorter, 'Cognitive fusion and defusion in acceptance and commitment therapy' (Guelph Therapist, no date), www.guelphtherapist.ca/blog/cognitive-fusion-defusion, accessed 30 October 2024

22 V Frankl, *Man's Search for Meaning: An introduction to logotherapy* (Beacon Press, 1959)

23 R Harris, *The Happiness Trap: Stop struggling, start living* (Robinson, 2012)

24 See, for example, B Shapero et al, 'Mindfulness-based interventions in psychiatry', *Focus*, 16/1 (Winter 2018), pp32–39, https://doi.org/10.1176/appi.focus.20170039; J Galante et al, 'Systematic review and individual participant data meta-analysis of randomized controlled trials assessing mindfulness-based programs for mental health promotion', *Nature Mental Health*, 1 (2023), pp462–476, https://doi.org/10.1038/s44220-023-00081-5; C Strauss

et al, 'Clinical effectiveness and cost-effectiveness of supported mindfulness-based cognitive therapy self-help compared with supported cognitive behavioral therapy self-help for adults experiencing depression', *JAMA Psychiatry*, 80/5 (2023), pp415–424, https://jamanetwork. com/journals/jamapsychiatry/fullarticle/2802550

25 B Katie, *Loving What Is: Four questions that can change your life* (Rider, 2002)

26 Letter from Vincent van Gogh to Theo van Gogh (28 October 1883), available at www.webexhibits.org// vangogh/letter/13/336.htm, accessed 12 May 2024

27 E Tolle, 'Accepting your unhappiness to be happy' (2 August 2022), www.youtube.com/ watch?v=9wd2CMXhU0s, accessed 19 September 2024

28 R Niebuhr, 'Serenity Prayer', l. 3

29 KA McLaughlin and S Nolen-Hoeksema, 'Rumination as a transdiagnostic factor in depression and anxiety', *Behaviour Research and Therapy*, 49/3 (March 2011), pp186–193, https://doi.org/10.1016/j.brat.2010.12.006

30 LC Michl et al, 'Rumination as a mechanism linking stressful life events to symptoms of depression and anxiety: Longitudinal evidence in early adolescents and adults', *Journal of Abnormal Psychology*, 122/2 (May 2013), pp339–352, https://doi.org/10.1037/a0031994

31 UK Rehab, 'Over-thinking is a danger in recovery' (UK Rehab, no date)

32 LM Hilt, A Aldao and K Fischer, 'Rumination and multi-modal emotional reactivity', *Cognition and Emotion*, 29/8 (2015), pp1486–1495, https://doi.org/10.1080/02699931.20 14.989816

33 V Pillai and C Drake, 'Sleep and repetitive thought: The role of rumination and worry in sleep disturbance', in: KA Babson and MT Feldner (eds) *Sleep and Affect* (Academic Press, 2015), pp201–225, https://doi.org/10.1016/B978-0-12-417188-6.00010-4

34 E Tolle (@EckhartTolle), 'Worry pretends to be useful' [X post] (7 May 2021), https://x.com/EckhartTolle/ status/1390705987938521091, accessed 22 May 2024

35 American Psychiatric Association, 'Rumination: A cycle of negative thinking' (APA, 5 March 2020), www.psychiatry. org/news-room/apa-blogs/rumination-a-cycle-of-negative-thinking, accessed 22 May 2024

36 M Cullen, 'How to regulate your emotions without suppressing them', *Greater Good Magazine* (30 January 2020), https://greatergood.berkeley.edu/article/item/how_to_regulate_your_emotions_without_suppressing_them, accessed 23 May 2024

37 S David, 'Recognizing your emotions as data, not directives' (Susan David, 20 July 2022), www.susandavid. com/newsletter/recognizing-your-emotions-as-data-not-directives, accessed 23 May 2024

38 Science Daily, 'Putting feelings into words produces therapeutic effects in the brain', *Science Daily* (22 June 2007), www.sciencedaily.com/releases/2007/06/070622090727. htm, accessed 24 May 2024

39 Mindfulness, 'How does mindfulness help with stress reduction? (+ 5 techniques to calm yourself)', *Mindfulness* (no date), https://mindfulness.com/stress/mindfulness-for-stress-reduction, accessed 24 May 2024

40 KD Neff, 'Self-compassion: Theory, method, research, and intervention', *Annual Review of Psychology*, 74 (2023), pp193–218, https://self-compassion.org/wp-content/uploads/2023/01/Neff-2023.pdf, accessed 24 May 2024

41 KD Neff, 'The role of self-compassion in development: A healthier way to relate to oneself', *Human Development*, 52/4 (June 2009), pp211–214, https://doi. org/10.1159/000215071

42 Mindfulness, 'Ease anxiety', *Mindfulness* (no date), https://mindfulness.com/anxiety, accessed 24 May 2024; MJ ter Avest et al, 'Interplay between self-compassion and affect during Mindfulness-Based Compassionate Living for recurrent depression: An autoregressive latent trajectory analysis', *Behaviour Research and Therapy*, 146 (November 2021), https://doi.org/10.1016/j.brat.2021.103946

43 O Winfrey, 'Oprah talks to Thich Nhat Hanh', *O, The Oprah Magazine* (March 2010), www.oprah.com/spirit/oprah-talks-to-thich-nhat-hanh, accessed 24 May 2024

44   Paul Ekman Group, 'What are emotions?' (Paul Ekman
     Group, no date), www.paulekman.com/universal-
     emotions, accessed 24 May 2024

45   MB Rosenberg, *Nonviolent Communication: A language of Life*
     (PuddleDancer, 2003)

46   TN Hanh, 'Go back and take care of yourself…'
     [Facebook post] (1 December 2016), www.facebook.
     com/thichnhathanh/posts/go-back-and-take-care-of-
     yourself-your-body-needs-you-your-feelings-need-you-
     you/10154349910279635, accessed 12 May 2024

47   See, for example, RJ Stanborough, 'What are cognitive
     distortions and how can you change these thinking
     patterns?', *Healthline* (25 October 2022), www.healthline.
     com/health/cognitive-distortions, accessed 25 May 2024

48   R Hanson, 'The brain: Velcro for the bad, Teflon for
     the good' (31 January 2020), www.youtube.com/
     watch?v=BwPvynau2oY, accessed 12 May 2024

49   J Li et al, 'Cognitive bias modification for adult's
     depression: A systematic review and meta-analysis',
     Frontiers in Psychology, 13 (December 2022), https://doi.
     org/10.3389/fpsyg.2022.968638

50   DO Hebb, *The Organization of Behavior: A neuropsychological
     theory* (John Wiley & Sons, 1949)

51   B Brown, 'The power of vulnerability' (TEDx Houston,
     June 2010), www.ted.com/talks/brene_brown_the_power_
     of_vulnerability, accessed 11 May 2024

52   R Ingber, 'Caregiver stress syndrome', *Today's Caregiver*
     (no date), https://caregiver.com/articles/caregiver-stress-
     syndrome, accessed 25 May 2024

53   Mental Health Foundation, 'What are the health benefits
     of altruism?' (MHF, no date), www.mentalhealth.org.uk/
     explore-mental-health/articles/what-are-health-benefits-
     altruism, accessed 25 May 2024

54   J Moll et al, 'Human fronto-mesolimbic networks guide
     decisions about charitable donation', *Proceedings of the
     National Academy of Sciences of the United States of America*,
     103/42 (17 October 2006), pp15623–15628, https://doi.
     org/10.1073/pnas.0604475103

55 B Taylor-Swaine, 'The science of kindness' (Bethan Taylor-Swaine, 21 May 2020), www.bethantaylorswaine.com/blog/the-science-of-kindness, accessed 25 May 2024

56 S Siegle, 'The art of kindness' (Mayo Clinic Health System, 17 August 2023), www.mayoclinichealthsystem.org/hometown-health/speaking-of-health/the-art-of-kindness, accessed 25 May 2024

57 DA Fryburg, 'Kindness as a stress reduction–health promotion intervention: A review of the psychobiology of caring', *American Journal of Lifestyle Medicine*, 16/1 (29 January 2021), pp89–100, https://doi.org/10.1177/1559827620988268

58 This quote is widely attributed to John Lennon but there is no definitive source or evidence for this.

59 M Manson, 'If you're so smart, why aren't you happy?' (Mark Manson, 17 July 2023), https://markmanson.net/breakthrough/031-if-youre-so-smart-why-arent-you-happy, accessed 12 May 2024

60 See, for example, R Harris, *ACT for adolescents* (2017), www.actmindfully.com.au/upimages/Making_Self-As-Context_Relevant,_Clear_and_Practical.pdf, accessed 19 September 2024; The IFS Institute, 'The Internal Family Systems model outline' (IFS Institute, no date), https://ifs-institute.com/resources/articles/internal-family-systems-model-outline, accessed 19 September 2024; SG Hofmann and AF Gómez, 'Mindfulness-based interventions for anxiety and depression', *Psychiatric Clinics of North America*, 40/4 (December 2017), pp739–749, https://doi.org/10.1016/j.psc.2017.08.008

61 See, for example, SL Shapiro et al, 'Cultivating mindfulness: Effects on well-being', *Journal of Clinical Psychology*, 64/7 (July 2008), pp840–862, https://doi.org/10.1002/jclp.20491; BR Parmentier et al, 'Mindfulness and symptoms of depression and anxiety in the general population: The mediating roles of worry, rumination, reappraisal and suppression', *Frontiers in Psychology*, 10/506 (8 March 2019), https://doi.org/10.3389/fpsyg.2019.00506

62 Mark Coleman, personal communication with the author

63 E Tolle, 'Life isn't as serious…' [Facebook post] (3 December 2020), www.facebook.com/Eckharttolle/photos/a.191110401216/10158768199161217/?type=3, accessed 12 May 2024

64 K Vogel, 'Understanding dispositional mindfulness', *PsychCentral* (6 July 2022), https://psychcentral.com/blog/dispositional-mindfulness-noticing-what-you-notice, accessed 5 June 2024

65 E Gilbert, *Letters from Love with Elizabeth Gilbert*, https://elizabethgilbert.substack.com, accessed 12 May 2024

66 L Vaughan-Lee, 'Oneness and Spiritual Ecology' (Working with Oneness, March 2013), https://workingwithoneness.org/articles/oneness-spiritual-ecology, accessed 27 May 2024

67 Vaughan-Lee, 'Oneness and Spiritual Ecology'

68 EO Wilson, *Consilience: The unity of knowledge* (Penguin Vintage, 1999)

69 D Attenborough, *David Attenborough: A Life on Our Planet* (Altitude Film Entertainment/Netflix, 2020)

70 Originally published as *Ein Psychologe erlebt das Konzentrationslager* (*A Psychologist Experiences the Concentration Camp*) (Verlag für Jugend und Volk, 1946)

71 Frankl, *Man's Search for Meaning*

72 N Mandela, *Long Walk to Freedom* (Little Brown & Co., 1994)

73 From a conversation with Richard Stengel (10 March 1993). Cited by the Nelson Mandela Foundation [Facebook post] (26 February 2014), www.facebook.com/NelsonMandelaCentreOfMemory/posts/prison-far-from-breaking-our-spirits-made-us-more-determined-to-continue-with-th/652011028170001, accessed 12 May 2024

74 N Mandela, 'I am prepared to die', *Nelson Mandela's Statement from the Dock at the Opening of the Defence Case in the Rivonia Trial* (20 April 1964). Available at www.un.org/en/events/mandeladay/court_statement_1964.shtml, accessed 12 May 2024

75 EK Hui and SK Tsang, 'Self-determination as a psychological and positive youth development construct', *Scientific World Journal* (2012), https://doi.org/10.1100/2012/759358

76 M Joshanloo, V Jovanović and J Park, 'Differential relationships of hedonic and eudaimonic well-being with self-control and long-term orientation', *Japanese Psychological Research*, 63/1 (January 2021), pp47–57, https://doi.org/10.1111/jpr.12276

77 RM Ryan and EL Deci, 'Self-determination theory and the facilitation of intrinsic motivation, social development, and well-being', *American Psychologist*, 55/1 (January 2000), pp68–78, https://selfdeterminationtheory.org/SDT/documents/2000_RyanDeci_SDT.pdf, accessed 28 May 2024

78 The origin of this quotation is unclear. SR Covey describes reading it in a book but cannot recall the author of the words. He describes this in the foreword to A Pattakos, *Prisoners of Our Thoughts: Viktor Frankl's principles for discovering meaning in life and work* (Berrett-Koehler Publishers, 2010), www.viktorfrankl.org/assets/pdf/Covey_Intro_to_Pattakos_Prisoners.pdf, accessed 28 May 2024

79 J Campbell, *The Hero with a Thousand Faces* (Pantheon Books, 1949)

80 Carl Jung first outlined the notion of the collective unconscious in his essay of 1916, 'The structure of the unconscious'. It was then further developed in his collection of essays, *The Archetypes and the Collective Unconscious*, published as Vol 9, Pt 1 of *The Collected Works of CG Jung* (Princeton University Press, 1969).

81 Campbell, *Hero with a Thousand Faces*

82 AK Schaffner, 'Understanding the circles of influence, concern, and control', *Positive Psychology* (1 June 2023), https://positivepsychology.com/circles-of-influence, accessed 30 May 2024

83 I Newton, Letter to Robert Hook (15 February 1676), available at https://digitallibrary.hsp.org/index.php/Detail/objects/9792, accessed 31 May 2024

Acknowledgements

'If I have seen further, it is because I am standing on
the shoulders of giants.'
— Isaac Newton[83]

I am privileged and deeply grateful to have been able
to gain guidance, insight, influence and support
over the years from some of the most inspirational,
talented, courageous and wise people. They range
from swamis, monks and mindfulness teachers to
neuroscientists, psychologists and researchers, as well
as the brave folk who I have had the honour of working with. Whether on retreats, courses and in coaching sessions, these are the people who have taken
the journey into deep resilience with me and showed
me what true strength is. A particular thank you to
all my beta participants who helped me develop the

Deep Resilience Experience course over the past few years: you helped me to fine-tune, hone and solidify this method.

To my teachers, mentors and guides: thank you. From the bottom of my heart, thank you. In my darkest hours, when I was younger and desperate for help, I was able to access your books, teachings, resources and support and that helped me find relief and stability, build my inner strength and then flourish. I'm only here today because you loved me into being.

Deep bow in gratitude to Eckhart Tolle, Adyashanti, Rupert Spira, Tara Brach, Jon Kabat-Zinn, Tony Robbins, Rick Hanson, Steven Hayes, Christopher Germer, Kristin Neff, Professor Paul Gilbert, Brené Brown, Jeff Foster, Gabor Mate. Thank you for your teachings.

Special thank you to Swami Kriyatama Saraswati (David Burgess). Thank you for believing in me, supporting me and taking me under your wing.

To Vidyamala Burch: you have impacted me more than you will ever know. Thank you for believing in me, supporting me, offering your incredible teachings and showing me an example of the kind of person I would like to be. The way you live your life is a lesson in itself and I have learned so much just from seeing who you are and how you treat people. If I can even partially reflect your positive impact, not just on me but on all those you meet, I will consider it an immense privilege.

To the lady who was teaching mindfulness in Tamworth when I was seventeen years old: I don't know your name but thank you. You changed my life. You may well have saved it.

Uncle Geoff: thank you for showing me what wisdom walking looks like. Your quiet and humble example has had a profound impact on me.

To my incredible friends and family: thank you for being my rock. I am beyond blessed to be surrounded by so much love.

To my mum: thank you for showing me that, no matter what happens to a person, no matter how hard, painful, scary or stressful, we don't have to let it define us. We can still rise strong and choose love.

The Author

Melli O'Brien is an internationally renowned educator and entrepreneur in the mental health space, specialising in mindfulness and resilience. Through her courses, retreats and app, she has helped over a million people globally, and she has been named by *Mindful* magazine as one of the most powerful women of the mindfulness movement.

Melli is the co-founder of Mindfulnes.com and The Mindfulness Summit, the world's largest mindfulness conference. Through these projects, she has donated over $750,000 dollars for mental health charities around the world.

She is the creator of the Deep Resilience Method, a trademarked method combining mindfulness with cutting-edge, evidence-based mental resilience skills that is aimed at helping people stay mentally strong during times of high stress or adversity.

Melli's own passion for teaching mental strength stems from her first-hand experience of overcoming depression and an eating disorder in her teens. After learning mindfulness at the age of seventeen she had a series of breakthroughs that radically changed the state of her mind and ultimately her entire life.

Melli has well and truly earned her reputation as a global leader in the field of mental strength. She is on a mission to make the world mentally stronger. Her big vision is to unlock the best in human potential, so we can work together to solve the world's most meaningful problems and create a more peaceful, equal and sustainable world.

⊕ https://melliobrien.com

◼ www.facebook.com/MelliOBrien

◉ @melliobrien

▶ www.youtube.com/@MelliOBrien

🎙 https://podcasts.apple.com/us/podcast/
deep-resilience/id1637748876

Made in the USA
Monee, IL
06 March 2025

13591487R00184